Series 6
Exam
SECRETS

Study Guide
Your Key to Exam Success

Series 6 Test Review for the
Investment Company Products
/Variable Contracts Limited
Representative Qualification Exam

Dear Future Exam Success Story:

Congratulations on your purchase of our study guide. Our goal in writing our study guide was to cover the content on the test, as well as provide insight into typical test taking mistakes and how to overcome them.

Standardized tests are a key component of being successful, which only increases the importance of doing well in the high-pressure high-stakes environment of test day. How well you do on this test will have a significant impact on your future, and we have the research and practical advice to help you execute on test day.

The product you're reading now is designed to exploit weaknesses in the test itself, and help you avoid the most common errors test takers frequently make.

How to use this study guide

We don't want to waste your time. Our study guide is fast-paced and fluff-free. We suggest going through it a number of times, as repetition is an important part of learning new information and concepts.

First, read through the study guide completely to get a feel for the content and organization. Read the general success strategies first, and then proceed to the content sections. Each tip has been carefully selected for its effectiveness.

Second, read through the study guide again, and take notes in the margins and highlight those sections where you may have a particular weakness.

Finally, bring the manual with you on test day and study it before the exam begins.

Your success is our success

We would be delighted to hear about your success. Send us an email and tell us your story. Thanks for your business and we wish you continued success.

Sincerely,

Mometrix Test Preparation Team

Need more help? Check out our flashcards at:
http://MometrixFlashcards.com/Series6

TABLE OF CONTENTS

Top 20 Test Taking Tips

1. Carefully follow all the test registration procedures
2. Know the test directions, duration, topics, question types, how many questions
3. Setup a flexible study schedule at least 3-4 weeks before test day
4. Study during the time of day you are most alert, relaxed, and stress free
5. Maximize your learning style; visual learner use visual study aids, auditory learner use auditory study aids
6. Focus on your weakest knowledge base
7. Find a study partner to review with and help clarify questions
8. Practice, practice, practice
9. Get a good night's sleep; don't try to cram the night before the test
10. Eat a well balanced meal
11. Know the exact physical location of the testing site; drive the route to the site prior to test day
12. Bring a set of ear plugs; the testing center could be noisy
13. Wear comfortable, loose fitting, layered clothing to the testing center; prepare for it to be either cold or hot during the test
14. Bring at least 2 current forms of ID to the testing center
15. Arrive to the test early; be prepared to wait and be patient
16. Eliminate the obviously wrong answer choices, then guess the first remaining choice
17. Pace yourself; don't rush, but keep working and move on if you get stuck
18. Maintain a positive attitude even if the test is going poorly
19. Keep your first answer unless you are positive it is wrong
20. Check your work, don't make a careless mistake

Regulatory Fundamentals and Business Development

Security

Security is defined as any note, stock, treasury stock, security future, security-based swap, bond, debenture, evidence of indebtedness, certificate of interest, or participation in any profit-sharing agreement, collateral-trust certificate, preorganization certificate or subscription, transferable share, investment contract, voting-trust certificate, certificate of deposit for a security, fractional undivided interest in oil, gas, or other mineral rights, any put, call, straddle, option, or privilege on any security, certificate of deposit, or group or index of securities, or any put, call, straddle, option, or privilege entered into on a national securities exchange relating to foreign currency, or, in general, any interest or instrument commonly known as a "security," or any certificate of interest or participation in, temporary or interim certificate for, receipt for, guarantee of, or warrant or right to subscribe to or purchase any of the foregoing.

Broker, dealer, and investment contract, and statutory disqualification

Dealer is defined as any person engaged in the business of buying and selling securities for his own account, through a broker or otherwise.
Investment Contract is defined as any contract, transaction, or scheme whereby a person invests money in a common enterprise and is led to expect profits solely from the efforts of the promoter or third party. Note that this vague definition has been the subject of a great deal of Supreme Court activity in the interpretation of whether or not certain transactions qualify as investment contracts, thus requiring registration.
One is subject to a statutory disqualification if such person (i) has been and is expelled or suspended from membership or participation with any member or self-regulatory organization, (ii) is subject to an order of the SEC denying, suspending, or revoking registration or barring or suspending association with a member, or (iii) has been found to be the cause of any suspension, expulsion, or order mentioned above.

FINRA

The Financial Industry Regulatory Authority (FINRA) is the largest independent regulator of securities firms in the United States. As stated on their website, "FINRA's mission is to protect America's investors by making sure the securities industry operates fairly and honestly." This mission is accomplished through a number of educational and regulatory tools, including all of the following:
1. Providing for the registration and education of all securities brokers

2. Conducting routine examinations of securities firms and their compliance with established procedures and record-keeping requirements
3. Monitoring trading on national securities exchanges
4. Developing new rules and regulations to react to changing market conditions and technology
5. Enforcing the rules and regulations, including the imposition of fines and civil and criminal penalties on violators
6. Providing a forum for arbitration and dispute resolution

Registration application and qualifications

FINRA's by-laws define persons eligible to become members and associated persons of members as "any registered broker, dealer, municipal securities broker or dealer, or government securities broker or dealer authorized to transact, and whose regular course of business consists in actually transacting, any branch of the investment banking or securities business in the United States, under the laws of the United States, shall be eligible for membership in the Corporation." There are exceptions to this eligibility rule, however, insofar as eligibility will be revoked if the member is subject to a disqualification or fails to continue to satisfy the filing requirements of the by-laws. The application membership must include an agreement to abide by the rules of all applicable federal and regulatory bodies, an agreement to pay dues and assessments as required, and any other such information required by the corporation.

Notification of termination and retention of jurisdiction

Within 30 days following the termination of an associated person, a member must give notice of the termination to FINRA. An additional copy of the notice provided to FINRA must also be provided to the terminated person. The provision within FINRA's by-laws relating to retention of jurisdiction simply means that even after a member or associated person has resigned or had membership canceled or revoked, that former member or associated person will still be subject to the filing of a complaint under FINRA's rules for any actions taken by the member or associated person prior to the resignation, cancellation or revocation of their membership. However, complaints may only be filed for up to 2 years following the effective date of the resignation, cancellation, or revocation.

NASD membership and registration

Membership application process

Pursuant to NASD Rule 1013, the new member application shall consist of the following information:
1. Form NMA
2. An original signed and notarized paper Form BD
3. An original FINRA-approved fingerprint card for each associated person
4. A new member assessment report
5. A detailed business plan, including financial statements, organizational chart, locations of businesses, types of securities to be offered, description

of sales practices, description of business facilities and copies of any lease or purchase agreements, and any other such information that may impact financial performance over the following 12 months

6. A description of any recent civil or criminal proceedings
7. A description of the record-keeping system to be utilized
8. A description of the supervisory system and procedures to be utilized
9. A description of the experience and qualifications of supervisors and registered principals
10. An agreement to abide by Firm Element continuing education requirements

<u>NASD Rule 1030</u>

NASD Rule 1030 provides that "persons associated with a member, including assistant officers other than principals, who are engaged in the investment banking or securities business for the member including the functions of supervision, solicitation, or conduct of business in securities or who are engaged in the training of persons associated with a member for any of these functions are designated as representatives." The rule provides for nine different categories of representatives, as follows:

1. General Securities Representative
2. Limited Representative – Investment Company and Variable Contracts Products
3. Limited Representative – Direct Participation Programs
4. Limited Representative – Options and Security Futures
5. Limited Representative – Corporate Securities
6. Limited Representative – Equity Trader
7. Limited Representative – Government Securities
8. Limited Representative – Private Securities Offerings
9. Limited Representative – Investment Banking

Regulated investment companies

As provided by Section 851 of the Internal Revenue Code, a regulated investment company is defined as a company that:

1. Files each year with its tax return an election to be considered a regulated investment company
2. Has at least 90 percent of its income derived from dividends, interest, payments with respect to securities loans, gains from the sale or other disposition of stock of securities or net income derived from an interest in a qualified publicly traded partnership
3. At the close of each quarter has at least 50 percent of its taxable assets represented by cash, government securities, and securities of other regulated investment companies, and all other securities are limited to having not more than 5 percent represented by any one issuer

Conduit theory

The conduit, or pipeline, theory states that companies such as regulated investment companies and real estate investment trusts are merely pass-through entities for capital gains, dividends, and interest of the securities in which they invest, and thus should not be taxed at the corporate level. The purpose of this theory is to avoid the overtaxation of income, which would reduce the value of securities to investors. For example, consider an equity security issued by Company A that is owned by regulated investment Company B. Investor C owns shares in Company B, and thereby realizes gains and losses from the capital appreciation and dividend payments of Company A's equity security. Company A's income is taxed at the corporate level and the remaining net income is used to reinvest in the company or pay dividends to equity shareholders. If it weren't for the pipeline theory, Company B would pay taxes on the dividends received. Then as the value of Company B's security increases as a result of the dividends paid by Company A, Investor C would be taxed on the growth of Company B's security. This double taxation is unnecessary because of the fact that the earnings are simply passed through Company B to Investor C, who ultimately bears the responsibility for paying taxes on gains and dividends.

Required distribution of income and realized capital gains

Pursuant to the Internal Revenue Code, a regulated investment company is required to distribute to its shareholders at least 90 percent of its gross investment company taxable income and at least 90 percent of its tax-exempt interest income. It is important to note that these requirements do not apply to capital gains. The purpose behind this requirement is that the regulated investment company is receiving preferential tax treatment in that it is not paying taxes on capital gains, dividends, and interest income and is only acting as a pass-through entity, so the investors in the regulated investment company will be the ones who ultimately pay the taxes. These distribution requirements ensure that the income is truly being passed through to investors and not held at the regulated investment company level, thereby being deferred until a later date and causing a reduction in current revenue for the IRS.

Taxation of capital gains and income

A regulated investment company pays taxes differently than normal companies. Regulated investment companies pay taxes only on an amount referred to as the investment company taxable income, which equals its taxable income offset by:
1. Capital gains
2. The amount of ordinary, taxable income distributed to its shareholders

Regulated investment companies are also taxed on their undistributed net capital gains and face an excise tax on certain amounts of undistributed income. Distributions from regulated investment companies are typically treated by shareholders as dividends of ordinary income, and thus taxed at dividend rates. However, a few exceptions do apply. For instance, if the regulated investment company pays a dividend but has no earnings and profits in a given year, the dividend is treated as a non-taxable return of capital, which will reduce a shareholder's cost basis.

FINRA By-Laws

<u>Article I – Definitions</u>
Act – Securities Exchange Act of 1934.
Board – the Board of Governors of the Corporation.
Closing – the closing of the consolidation of certain member firm regulatory functions of NYSE Regulation, Inc. and the Corporation.
Commission – the Securities and Exchange Commission.
Corporation – National Association of Securities Dealers, Inc. or any future name of the entity.
Delegation plan – the Plan of Allocation and Delegation of Functions by NASD to Subsidiaries.
District – a district established by the NASD Regulation Board.
Floor member governor – a member of the Board who is associated with a member specialist or floor broker on the NYSE trading floor.
Governor – member of the Board.
Independent dealer/insurance affiliate governor – a member of the board associated with a member who is an independent contractor financial planning member firm or insurance company.
Industry director – a director of the NASD Regulation Board who has served in the previous year as on officer or has a consulting employment relationship with a self regulatory organization.
Industry governor – the floor member governor, independent dealer/insurance affiliate governor, and investment company affiliate governor and any other governor who has served in the previous year as an officer, or has a consulting employment relationship with a self regulatory organization.
Investment company affiliate governor – member of the Board associated with an investment company member.
Joint public governor – the public governor to be appointed by the Board of Directors of the NYSE Group, Inc. and the Board in office prior to the closing jointly.
Large firm – a broker/dealer member with 500 or more registered persons.
Large firm governor – a member of the board to be elected by large firm members.
Large firm governor committee – a committee of the Board comprised of all the large firm governors.
Lead governor – a member of the Board elected as such.
Mid-size firm – any broker/dealer member with at least 151, and no more than 499, registered persons.
Mid-size firm governor – a member of the board elected by mid-size firm members.
Member – any broker/dealer admitted to membership in the Corporation.
NASD group committee – a committee of the Board comprised of the five public governors, the independent dealer/insurance affiliate governor, and the small firm governors.
NASD public governors – the five public governors appointed as such.

NYSE group committee – a committee of the Board comprised of the five public governors, the floor member governor, and the large firm governors nominated by the NYSE Group Inc.

NYSE public governors – the five public governors appointed by the Board of Directors of NYSE Group, Inc.

Public director – a director of the NASD Regulation Board.

Public governor – a governor or committee member who is not the CEO of the Corporation.

Small firm – and broker/dealer member with 1 to 150 registered persons.

Small firm governor – a member of the Board elected by small firm members.

Small firm governor committee – a committee of the Board comprised of all the small firm governors.

Article III – Qualifications of members and associated persons

Persons eligible to become members and associated persons of members (Section 1) - any registered broker, dealer, municipal securities broker or dealer, or government securities broker or dealer can be members. Any person can be an associated person of a member, unless otherwise ineligible.

Authority of Board to adopt qualification requirements (Section 2) - the Board has the authority to adopt rules and regulations applicable to applicants.

Ineligibility of certain persons for membership or association (Section 3) - no registered broker, dealer, municipal securities broker or dealer, or government securities broker or dealer can be a member if he fails to satisfy the qualification requirements. No person can be associated with a member if the person does not meet the qualification requirements. The Board has the authority to cancel a person's membership. If a member is found to be ineligible, the member can file an application for relief with the Board.

Definition of disqualification (Section 4) - a person is disqualified in regards to membership if the person is subject to a statutory disqualification.

Article V – Registered representatives and associated persons

Qualification requirements (Section 1) - a member is not to permit an associated person to engage in investment banking or securities business unless such person meets the qualification requirements.

Application for registration (Section 2) - a signed application for membership is to be submitted electronically and is to contain:
A. an agreement to comply with governing laws, rules, and regulations;
B. other reasonable information required by the Corporation.

Notification by member to the Corporation and associated person of termination; amendments to notification (Section 3) - if a member terminates an associated person, the member is to give notice to the Corporation within 30 days, and give a copy of the same notice to the person terminated. If the member finds any facts in such notice to be incomplete or inaccurate, the member is to file an amendment and submit it to the Corporation with a copy to the person terminated within 30 days of first learning of the facts.

Retention of jurisdiction (Section 4) - a person who has had his association with a member terminated is still subject to filing a complaint based upon conduct that began prior to termination.

Electronic filing requirements

The enumerated uniform forms are to be filed electronically. A member is to identify a registered principal with authority over registration functions to be responsible for the supervision of the electronic filing of forms. The electronic filing of a Form U4 is to be based on a manually signed Form U4 by the person on whose behalf the form is being filed, though amendments to the Form can be filed electronically without a manually signed form needed. Fingerprint information is to be sent to FINRA within 30 days of the Form U4 filing, or the registration will be deemed inactive. Initial filing and amendments of Form U5 are to be filed electronically.

Filing of misleading information as to membership or registration

Filing of misleading information as to membership or registration (FINRA Rule 1122) - a member may not file information with FINRA having to do with membership or registration that is incomplete or accurate so as to be misleading. If a member does so, it is to be immediately corrected.

Failure to register personnel (NASD IM-1000-3) - if a member fails to register an employee as a registered representative who should be so registered it is found to be conduct inconsistent with just and equitable principles of trade, and may be cause for disciplinary action.

Branch offices and offices of supervisory jurisdiction (NASD IM-1000-4) - a member is required to ensure that its membership application is kept current by means of supplementary amendments and to ensure that the main office is properly designated and registered, if required. A member is required to designate offices of supervisory jurisdiction, and must register those branch offices.

Continuing education requirements

FINRA Rule 1250 establishes the need for continuing education for a FINRA licensed broker. Unless otherwise instructed, individuals must complete their continuing education requirements within 120 days of the second anniversary of holding their license. Failure to complete the continuing education requirements results in having one's license put into inactive status until brought up to date. The continuing

- 8 -

education may be provided by the firm that the broker works for, provided that certain elements are in place. This includes the following:
The firm has a designated principal or officer in charge
The delivery takes place at a site under the control of the firm
The continuing education is supervised by a proctor
The sites are made available to FINRA for examination
A letter of attestation is sent to the designated examining authority (DEA) detailing items 1-4 above

Arbitration disclosure to associated persons signing or acknowledging form U4

Form U4 contains a pre-dispute arbitration clause in item five of Section 15A. It states that most or all disputes must be resolved in arbitration if no agreement is reached in the less binding mediation. When registered representatives sign their Form U4, under item five of Section 15A, they relinquish the right to sue another legal person unless the arbitration declares that they may. Item five further states that alleged discrimination is not covered under the arbitration rules of FINRA, and legal resolution may be sought in another manner. Similarly to discrimination, whistleblowers that have a dispute with their employer are not required to settle the matter under arbitration. Further, the arbitrator's decision is final, with limited opportunity to appeal, and arbitrators are not required to explain the reasoning behind their decisions.
In addition to registered individuals being subject to pre-dispute clauses, many FINRA members now require their customers to sign pre-dispute clauses as part of the application process. This allows all customer disputes to be settled in arbitration.

Outside business activities of registered persons

Pursuant to the rules established in FINRA Rule 3270 Outside Business Activities of Registered Persons, no registered person may serve as an employee, independent contractor, sole proprietor, officer, director, or be compensated from any other person as a result of work done outside of the scope of relationship with his or her member firm without prior written approval from the registered person's member firm. It is up to the member firm to specify the written form in which this prior approval must be received. In determining whether or not to permit the outside business activities, the member should consider whether the activities will interfere with the registered person's obligations to the member and how customers will react to the activities, including whether they might view the outside activities as being part of the registered person's role with the member firm.

Reporting requirements

Under FINRA Rule 4530, FINRA member firms should report violations within 30 calendar days of their occurrence. Part B of Rule 4530 allows the member time to

- 9 -

determine that an actual violation has occurred and specifies the firm "to report to FINRA within 30 calendar days after the firm has concluded, or reasonably should have concluded, on its own that the firm or an associated person of the firm has violated any securities, insurance, commodities, financial or investment-related laws, rules, regulations or standards of conduct of any domestic or foreign regulatory body or self-regulatory organization." Rule 4530 further goes on to state that customer "statistical and summary information" regarding customer complaints should be filed each quarter by the 15th calendar day following the end of the quarter.

Some FINRA members create their own reporting guidelines, but these guidelines must always be at least as frequent as those outlined in Rule 4530. Many members set up stricter reporting guidelines. Following stricter reporting dates will help prevent the registered person from violating FINRA rules.

Registration requirements

Registration requirements (NASD Rule 1031) - any person engaged as a representative in the investment banking or securities business of a member must be registered. In order to be registered, he must pass a Qualification Examination according to their category of registration. A representative is defined as a person associated with a member including assistant officers other than principals, involved in the investment banking or securities business including functions such as supervision, solicitation, and training. If a person's registration has lapsed for two or more years, the person is required to retake a Qualification Examination for Representatives corresponding to his registration.

Persons exempt from registration

NASD Rule 1060 provides for four circumstances under which a person associated with a member may be exempt from registration with the NASD, as follows:
Persons associated with a member whose functions are solely and exclusively clerical or ministerial;
Persons associated with a member who are not actively engaged in the investment banking or securities business;
Persons associated with a member whose functions are related solely and exclusively to the member's need for nominal corporate officers or for capital participation; and
Persons associated with a member whose functions are related solely and exclusively to (i) effecting transactions on the floor of a national securities exchange and who are registered as floor members with such exchange, (ii) transactions in municipal securities, (iii) transactions in commodities, or (iv) transactions in security futures, provided that any such person is registered with a registered futures association.

Qualification examinations and waiver of requirements

Qualification examinations and waiver of requirements (NASD Rule 1070) - Qualification Examinations are a series of questions based on topic outlines from the Association. Results from such examinations are given to the member firms. In certain cases, NASD may waive the requirement of a Qualification Examination in lieu of other standard acceptable as proof of qualification. If a person fails the examination, he may take it again after 30 days, unless he has failed three times, in which case he must wait a period of 180 days.

Confidentiality of examinations (NASD Rule 1080) - the Qualification Examinations are confidential. An exam is not to be removed from the examination center, and any reproduction, disclosure, or receipt of any portion of the exam is prohibited.

Confidentiality of examinations

NASD Rule 1080 provides important guidance around the confidentiality of NASD examinations. Actions that are considered to violate this confidentiality and are thus prohibited include removal of the exam from the exam center, reproduction of the exam, and receiving from or providing to anyone else any information contained in the exam. Candidates who sit for exams must not receive any assistance when taking the exam and must certify that they neither received nor provided any type of assistance.
The NASD takes confidentiality of the exams very seriously as it is critically important to their mission of protecting investors and maintaining a secure and efficient securities market to have knowledgeable and competent representatives throughout the securities industry who are well versed in the rules and regulations surrounding their actions. Any violation of the confidentiality of the exams threatens to undermine the quality and efficacy of this regulation.

Supervision

NASD Rule 3010 Supervision provides specific guidance for member firms with respect to the supervisory systems and written procedures that must be maintained. A member's supervisory system must provide for the establishment and maintenance of written procedures that:
  i.   Include the designation of an appropriately registered principal who has the authority to carry out the supervisory responsibilities of the member for each type of business in which it engages and for which registration as a broker/dealer is required

ii.   Designation of offices of supervisory jurisdiction (OSJ), considering whether registered persons at the location engage in retail sales or other interaction with public customers, whether a substantial number of registered persons conduct business from that location, whether the location is separated geographically from another OSJ, whether the member's registered persons are geographically dispersed, and whether the securities at the location are complex and/or diverse.

Additionally, each registered person must be assigned to a registered representative or principal who will be responsible for supervising that person's activities, the member firm must make reasonable efforts to ensure that all supervisory personnel are qualified to carry out their duties, and each registered representative and registered principal must take part in a meeting to discuss relevant compliance matters at least once annually.

Internal investigations
Pursuant to NASD Rule 3010 Supervision, "Each member shall conduct a review, at least annually, of the businesses in which it engages, which review shall be reasonably designed to assist in detecting and preventing violations of, and achieving compliance with, applicable securities laws and regulations, and with applicable NASD rules." During each investigation, member firms should review the activities of each office of supervisory jurisdiction and any branch office that supervises one or more non-branch locations. The topics that must be covered in the written report of the internal investigation include: safeguarding of customer funds and securities, maintaining books and records, supervision of customer accounts serviced by branch office managers, transmittal of funds between customers and registered representatives and between customers and third parties, validation of customer address changes and validation of changes in customer account information.

Office of Supervisory Jurisdiction and Branch Office
NASD Rule 3010 defines an Office of Supervisory Jurisdiction, or OSJ, as "any office of a member at which any one or more of the following functions take place:
   a.   Order execution and/or market making
   b.   Structuring of public offerings or private placements
   c.   Maintaining custody of customers' funds and/or securities
   d.   Final acceptance (approval) of new accounts on behalf of the member
   e.   Review and endorsement of customer orders, pursuant to paragraph (d) above
   f.   Final approval of retail communications for use by persons associated with the member, pursuant to FINRA Rule 2210(b)(1), except for an office that solely conducts final approval of research reports
   g.   Responsibility for supervising the activities of persons associated with the member at one or more other branch offices of the member"

NASD Rule 3010 defines a Branch Office as "any location where one or more associated persons of a member regularly conducts the business of effecting any transactions in, or inducing or attempting to induce the purchase or sale of any security, or is held out as such."

Private securities transactions of an associated person

According to NASD Rule 3040, which governs the private securities transactions of an associated person, an associated person must provide written notice detailing the proposed private securities transaction prior to participating in any private securities transaction. Additionally, the written notice must describe the associated person's role in the transaction and disclose whether or not any selling compensation may be received as a result of the proposed transaction. If the transactions may result in selling compensation, the member firm must either approve or disapprove the person's participation and, if approved, the transaction will be recorded on the books of the member firm and the member shall supervise the person's activities as if the transaction were executed on behalf of the member. If the member disapproves the transaction, then the person may not participate, directly or indirectly, in the transaction.

Rule 156 of the Securities Act of 1933

Pursuant to Rule 156 of the Securities Act of 1933, there are 2 requirements related to material facts. The first requirement is that investment company sales literature may not contain an untrue statement of material fact. Additionally, investment company sales literature may not omit to state a material fact that is necessary in order to make a statement made not misleading. Each circumstance is considered within the context in which the statement is made, and will be evaluated in conjunction with other statements made in connection with the sale of the same security and the absence of other explanations or qualifications that are necessary to make a statement not misleading, among others. Potential investors need to be made aware of all materials facts related to an investment company security to allow them to make an informed investment decision.

Omission of a material fact
One example of an omission of a material fact could be in the presentation of performance information. For instance, an investment company's past returns could have been primarily driven by one investment in a small-cap company that significantly outperformed the rest of the market. Without that security, the fund may have significantly underperformed its peers and this needs to be communicated to potential investors to provide accurate information from which to make an informed decision. Another omission of a material fact would be an instance in which an investment company recently had significant turnover among senior executives and long-tenured portfolio managers. Without this information, an investor may believe that the same managers who had achieved the past performance of the company would be the same individuals managing the company

moving forward. However, this is not the case and potential investors must be made aware of this.

<u>Untrue statement of material fact</u>
One example of an untrue statement of material fact would be the case of a company who discloses past performance based on back-testing of their current portfolio holdings. For instance, assume an investment company had returned 3% to investors over the past five years. However, they recently implemented a new portfolio management strategy and the back-tested results of their new portfolio holdings show that this portfolio would have yielded 12% annually over the prior five years. The company chooses to report this performance as their historical performance in their prospectus and sales literature, thereby leading investors to think they had actually achieved these returns for shareholders. Another example is in the case of the qualifications of portfolio managers and company management. Assume that an investment company has stated in its sales literature that all of its portfolio managers have earned the CFA charter. In fact, several of the managers have passed the exams but have not yet been granted the charter. This would lead potential investors to believe that the portfolio managers are more qualified than they actually might be.

Investment Company Act of 1940

<u>Section 30</u>
As outlined in Section 30 of the Investment Company Act of 1940, registered investment companies must periodically provide the following:

  i.   such information, documents, and reports as the Commission may require to keep reasonably current the information and documents in the registration statement of such company
  ii. copies of every periodic or interim report or similar communication containing financial statements and transmitted to any class of such company's security holders within 10 days of such transmission
  iii. reports to the company's shareholders at least semiannually containing a balance sheet, amounts and values of securities owned, an income statement, a surplus statement, a report of all remuneration paid to directors and officers, and a statement of the aggregate purchases and sales of investment securities made during the reporting period.

<u>Section 35</u>
Section 35 of the Investment Company Act of 1940 states the following: It shall be unlawful for any person, issuing or selling any security of which a registered investment company is the issuer, to represent or imply in any manner whatsoever that such security or company (A) has been guaranteed, sponsored, recommended, or approved by the United States, or any agency, instrumentality, or officer of the United States, (B) has been insured by the Federal Deposit Insurance Corporation, or (C) is guaranteed by or is otherwise an obligation of any bank or insured

depository institution. The decision as to whether or not a name is misleading is ultimately made by the Commission.

One way in which an investment company could utilize a misleading name is to imply that the investment company has been sponsored by, or is backed by, the United States government. An example of such an investment company name would be the "United States Treasury Investment Company." Another method of misleading investors is to imply that the company or the fund has been insured by the FDIC. This is particularly troublesome for investment companies with strong ties to banking institutions. An example would be the "ABC Bank Fund–FDIC Insured." A third misleading investment company name would be one that implies that it has been guaranteed by a bank or other depository institution, such as the "ABC Bank Guaranteed Interest Fund." Finally, investment companies should avoid certain phrases in their names that indicate some guarantee of performance if that is not strictly provided. For instance, the "ABC Fixed Rate Fund," when in fact the fund provides a highly variable rate.

Accounts and records, reports, examinations of exchanges, members, and others

Under Rule 17(f)(2) of the Securities Exchange Act of 1934, all partners, directors, officers, and employees of every member of a national securities exchange, broker, dealer, registered transfer agent, and registered clearing agency are required to be fingerprinted. The fingerprints are submitted to the United States Attorney General to be processed and maintained on file. There are some exceptions to this rule, however, such as employees who are not engaged in the sale of securities, employees who do not have regular access or do not regularly process securities or cash, and employees who do not have direct supervisory responsibility for employees with the responsibilities previously described.
The importance of this requirement lies in the ability that it provides for the United States government and regulatory organizations to identify members' employees and to help prevent fraudulent activity.

Section 15A of the Securities Exchange Act of 1934

Section 15A of the Securities Exchange Act of 1934 established the NASD (now FINRA). As stated by FINRA, their mission statement is as follows: "FINRA is dedicated to investor protection and market integrity through effective and efficient regulation of the securities industry." FINRA is the largest independent regulator of the financial markets and serves a number of purposes including protecting investors from fraud, examining broker and dealer firms, enforcing securities laws, registering, testing, and educating brokers, reviewing sales materials and communications to investors, educating investors and resolving disputes between brokers and investors. FINRA enforces rules and laws through its ability to bar individuals from association with member firms, to suspend brokers from association with member firms, and to levy fines and order restitution in cases of significant financial loss as a result of fraud or unethical sales practices.

Investment Advisers Act of 1940

The Investment Advisers Act of 1940 is intended to provide additional regulation for investment advisers, as such advisers are considered to provide advice and counsel through means of interstate commerce, the advice and counsel of such companies typically relates to the purchase and sale of securities on a national securities exchange or through the Federal Reserve system, and the volume of such transactions is significant enough to have a direct impact on interstate commerce, national securities exchange, the national banking system and the national economy. The Act was largely the result of the stock market crash in 1929, which wiped out the savings of millions. As a result, the government felt the need to regulate the advice, counsel, and analyses provided to investors by investment advisers.

Investment adviser

Under the Investment Advisers Act of 1940, "investment adviser" is defined as "any person who, for compensation, engages in the business of advising others, either directly or through publications or writings, as to the value of securities or as to the advisability of investing in, purchasing, or selling securities, or who, for compensation and as part of a regular business, issues or promulgates analyses or reports concerning securities." This definition does not include:
1. A bank or bank-holding company
2. Any lawyer, accountant, engineer, or teacher whose performance of investment services is incidental to his professional practice
3. Any broker or dealer, provided that the services performed are incidental to the regular business as a broker or dealer and from which the broker or dealer receives no special compensation
4. The publishers of newspapers, news magazines, or business and financial publications
5. Those whose advice only concerns securities that are direct obligations of the United States
6. Any nationally recognized statistical rating organization
7. Any family office
8. Anyone else as designated by the Securities Exchange Commission

Person associated with an investment adviser

According to the Investment Advisers Act of 1940, person associated with an investment adviser shall refer to "any partner, officer, or director of such investment adviser (or any person performing similar functions), or any person directly or indirectly controlling or controlled by such investment adviser, including any employee of such investment adviser." It is important to note that those employees of an investment adviser who serve in only clerical or ministerial roles are not considered to be persons associated with an investment adviser. The ability to determine who is "associated" under this regulation is important because it is that distinction that determines an individual's requirements under the Act and the potential civil and criminal penalties one could face as a result of a violation of the Act.

Information to apply for registration

In order to register with the Securities Exchange Commission as an investment adviser, one must file the following information:

1. The name and form of organization under which the investment adviser engages or intends to engage in business
2. The name of the state under which the investment adviser is organized
3. The location of the principal office and branch locations
4. The names and addresses of any partners, officers, and directors
5. The number of employees
6. The education and past and present business affiliations of all partners, directors, and officers
7. The nature of business of the investment adviser
8. A balance sheet certified by an independent public accountant and other financial statements
9. The nature and scope of the investment adviser's authority with respect to client accounts
10. The basis for compensation
11. Whether the investment adviser is subject to a disqualification
12. A statement as to whether the primary scope of business for the investment adviser is acting as an investment adviser or rendering investment supervisory services

Companies exempt from registration

The Investment Advisers Act of 1940 provides for exemption from registration for a few certain types of companies. For example, investment advisers that provide advice solely to venture capital funds are required to be registered under the Act. Additionally, investment advisers to private funds with less than $150 million assets under management are also exempt from registration. However, these investment advisers to private funds are required by the Act to provide reporting to the Commission to ensure that the public interest and its investors are sufficiently protected. As shown by these two examples, the Act is less concerned with the protection of sophisticated private investors and venture capital firms than with investment advice that is provided to less sophisticated investors without the resources to conduct the same level of due diligence for themselves. Scrutiny under the act increases with the size of the transaction, the complexity of the security, and the lower the sophistication of the customer.

Impact of Securities Act of 1933 on marketing and prospecting regulations

The Securities Act of 1933, which is also sometimes known as the "truth in securities" act, was designed with two objectives in mind: (i) that investors are provided with all relevant information about any securities that are offered for sale and (ii) to prohibit fraudulent activities throughout the marketing and sale of securities. More specifically, the act requires securities to be registered with the Securities Exchange Commission. Some of the information that must be provided for the registration includes a description of the issuer's business, a description of the security being marketed, information regarding the issuer's management team, and certified financial statements of the issuer. Additionally, the act prohibits issuers, brokers, dealers, and other parties involved in the marketing and sale of securities from misrepresenting the features of the security or the financial status of the issuing company.

Interstate commerce or mail system for selling securities

Section 5 of the Securities Exchange Act of 1933 sets forth several rules and prohibitions with respect to the use of interstate commerce and the mail service in selling securities. Specifically, the act prohibits the use of interstate commerce or the mail system to sell any security that does not have a registration statement in place. It also prohibits the sale of a security or the delivery of a prospectus unless the prospectus of such security conforms to Section 10 of the Securities Exchange Act of 1933. Finally, securities cannot be offered for sale if the registration statement is the subject of a refusal order or a stop order prior to the registration date. These requirements do not apply in the case of emerging companies who are in discussions with qualified institutional investors or accredited investors.

Prospectus requirements

Pursuant to Section 10 of the Securities Act of 1933, the prospectus must be submitted along with the registration statement for a security, but is not deemed to be part of that registration statement. Upon submission, the registrations statement of the security is effective the twentieth day after filing, or earlier if approved by the Commission. Also contained in Section 10 of the 1933 Act is language regarding the timing requirements for information contained in the prospectus, which states that "when a prospectus is used more than nine months after the effective date of the registration statement, the information continued therein shall be as of a date not more than sixteen months prior to such use." This is to help ensure that investors are being provided with current and relevant information that can be used in their investment decision-making process.

Civil liabilities

Section 11 of the Securities Act of 1933 provides purchases of securities with an avenue for pursuing civil liabilities as a result of fraudulent activities. Specifically, investors are granted the opportunity to pursue civil liabilities when they have unknowingly purchased a security that contained in its registration statement an untrue statement of material fact or an omission of material fact that would be required to make the statements in the registration statement not misleading to the investor. More specifically, the investor would have the opportunity to sue anyone who signed the registration statement, anyone who was a director or partner in the issuer at the time of filing the registration, every person who is currently or about to be named a director, every underwriter of the security, and every accountant, engineer, or appraiser whose statement in such a registration statement is the subject of the fraudulent activity.

Section 11 of the Securities Act of 1933 provides that an investor who has purchased a security that in its registration statement contained an untrue statement or omission of material fact may sue signers of the securities registration statement, directors and partners of the company (both at the time of registration and current), underwriters associated with the distribution of the security, and professionals who gave opinions in the registration statement that led to the untrue claims or omissions of fact. The suit to recover damages equal to the difference between the amount paid for the security and either (i) the values of the security at such time the suit was brought, (ii) the price at which the security was sold in the market before the suit was brought, or (iii) the price at which the security will be sold after the suit was brought but before damages have been determined.

Fraudulent interstate transaction

As provided in Section 17 of the Securities Act of 1933, "It shall be unlawful for any person in the offer or sale of any securities (including security-based swaps) or any security-based swap agreement by the use of any means or instruments of transportation or communication in interstate commerce or by use of the mails, directly or indirectly:
1. To employ any device, scheme, or artifice to defraud, or
2. To obtain money or property by means of any untrue statement of a material fact or any omission to state a material fact necessary in order to make the statements made, in light of the circumstances under which they were made, not misleading, or
3. To engage in any transaction, practice, or course of business which operates or would operate as a fraud or deceit upon the purchaser.

No approval clause

Section 23 of the Securities Act of 1933, often referred to as the "no approval clause," is meant to indicate to investors that while the SEC is responsible for approving the registration of a security, they are in no way responsible for the truth and accuracy of the registration statement and do not warrant the security as being a good investment. The act reads as follows: "Neither the fact that the registration statement for a security has been filed or is in effect nor the fact that a stop order is not in effect with respect thereto shall be deemed a finding by the Commission that registration statement is true and accurate on its face or that it does not contain an untrue statement of fact or omit to state a material fact, or be held to mean that the Commission has in any way passed upon the merits of, or given approval to, such security. It shall be unlawful to make, or cause to be made, to any prospective purchaser any representation contrary to the foregoing provisions of this section."

Prospectus and statement of additional information

The purpose of the prospectus is to ensure that investors have access and are provided with, prior to the purchase of a security, a minimal level of information that is necessary for the investment decision-making process. Such information within the prospectus includes a mutual fund's objectives, strategy, risks, fees and expenses, and past performance. The format of each prospectus is the same to enable investors to easily compare different investments. The Statement of Additional Information is meant to provide additional information to assist in the investment-making decision that is not typically available, or required to be contained, within the prospectus. Such information may include detailed information about the fund's investment advisers and information relating to the purchasing and redemption of shares. This additional information may be useful to certain investors looking at detailed nuances between similar investments or who are concerned about certain information within the prospectus and want to seek additional information.

The Securities Act of 1933 provides that any advertisements must notify investors of how to obtain additional information such as the prospectus and statement of additional information and urges investors to consider all of the facts and circumstances of the investment product prior to making a decision. The additional information will be critical to the investment decision because the prospectus provides information such as a mutual fund's objectives, strategy, risks, fees and expenses, and past performance. The format of each prospectus is the same to enable investors to easily compare different investments. Additionally, the Statement of Additional Information (SAI) includes detailed information about the fund's investment advisers and information relating to the purchasing and redemption of shares. This additional information may be useful to certain investors looking at detailed nuances between similar investments or who are concerned about certain information within the prospectus and want to seek additional information.

Offer to sell and prospectus

The Securities Act of 1933 defines offer to sell as including "every attempt or offer to dispose of, or solicitation of an offer to buy, a security or interest in a security, for value." However, the act does further clarify that an offer to sell does not include preliminary negotiations or agreements between an issuer and an underwriter who are in contract with an issuer. The act defines prospectus as "any prospectus, notice, circular, advertisement, letter, or communication, written or by radio or television, which offers any security for sale or confirms the sale of any security." The act goes on to clarify that a notice, circular, letter, or advertisement is not considered to be a prospectus so long as it states from whom a prospectus can be obtained and does not do any more than identify the security and the price and state from which orders will be executed.

Prospectus information

The purpose of the prospectus is to ensure that investors have access and are provided with, prior to the purchase of a security, a minimal level of information that is necessary for the investment decision-making process. Such information within the prospectus includes a mutual fund's objectives, strategy, risks, fees and expenses, and past performance. The format of each prospectus is the same to enable investors to easily compare different investments. An understanding of the fund's objectives is important to a potential investor because there is variation, even within the same asset class and style, as to how the fund seeks to meet its investment objectives. Freedom to permit allocations to other styles and to use risk management techniques and derivatives can play a significant role in a fund's performance and will be outlined in the prospectus where the fund's strategy is described.

Investment objectives, policies, and restrictions

A security's prospectus must include certain relevant information related to the fund's investment objectives, policies and asset allocation, or risk management restrictions. Typically, the prospectus contains a brief sentence or paragraph explaining the overarching objective of the fund. For instance, one objective might be "to achieve maximum total long-term return by investing in investment grade debt securities of varying maturities." The prospectus will also include several paragraphs outlining the specific strategy employed, and any restrictions in place, in order to achieve the stated objective. For instance, a fixed income fund may be required to maintain at least an 80% allocation to fixed income securities in order to stay true to its asset class and style. However, that same fund may also be limited to not investing more than 20% of its assets into high-yield fixed income instruments. All of this information is critically important in helping an investor to evaluate the fund.

Sales loads and fees and share classes

A security's prospectus must include certain relevant information related to the fund's sales loads, fees, and share classes. The mutual fund prospectus will include a detailed table showing the applicable fees, in percentages, for each available share class. Fees may include maximum sales charge loads, management fees, distribution and service fees (12b-1), and other expenses that are part of the cost of operating the fund. In some circumstances, there may also be potential credits to the investor such as fee waivers, expense reimbursements, or breakpoints for large purchases. Any such discounts or waivers will also be detailed in this section of the prospectus. Following the table of charges, there will also be an example showing the total expenses for each share class over a given period of time and assuming to have earned a hypothetical rate of return. The fee and share class information is very important for investors to review carefully as it will directly impact an investor's returns.

Breakpoints, rights of accumulation, combinations of accounts, and letters of intent

A security's prospectus must include certain relevant information related to each share class's breakpoints, rights of accumulation, combination of accounts, and letters of intent. Some funds may offer "breakpoints," or reduced sales loads, as the size of your investment increases. The prospectus provides the investor with additional information as to whether this is available for a given share class and, if so, at what size the breakpoint would take effect. Another way for investors to capitalize on reduced sales loads is through rights of accumulation. If the prospectus offers this option, all accounts owned by family members living at the same address can be combined and considered in reducing the sales loads on a new purchase. Finally, an investor does not necessarily have to invest the full amount immediately. If provided in the prospectus, an investor may be able to submit a letter of intent to the fund company stating the amount that they intend to purchase in a given period of time. Sales loads would then be based upon this higher investment.

Limitations on methods of sale

The mutual fund prospectus must provide the potential investor with necessary information on how to acquire shares of the fund. This may include through an authorized intermediary or distributor, by mail, by telephone, online, by bank wire, or by ACH. For each transaction, the prospectus will include instructions as to how to complete the transaction. In addition to the various methods of purchase, the prospectus will contain additional information regarding the fund pricing and net asset value calculations as well as additional information regarding the costs to open various accounts and the types of personal information that will be required upon purchase. All of this information is meant to ensure that an investor knows all of the available options with regard to methods by which he can purchase shares of the mutual fund.

Limitations on methods of redemption

The mutual fund prospectus must provide the investor with necessary information on how to redeem shares of the fund. This may include through an authorized intermediary or distributor, by mail, by telephone, online, by bank wire, or by ACH. For each transaction, the prospectus will include instructions as to how to complete the transaction. In addition to the various methods of redemption, the prospectus will contain additional information regarding the fund pricing and net asset value calculations as well as any options available to investors with respect to exchanging shares of the fund for other shares within the same fund family. Oftentimes this can result in reduced sales load for the investor, although he would still be subject to the taxation of any realized gains. All of this information is meant to ensure that an investor knows all of the available options with regard to methods by which he can redeem shares of the mutual fund.

Financial statement information

A security's prospectus must contain certain relevant information to assist an investor in his investment decision-making process. However, specific financial statement information is not required to be included in either the summary

- 22 -

prospectus or the more detailed statutory prospectus. Instead, funds must only disclose certain "financial highlights" within the prospectus and the detailed financial statement information will be provided within the Statement of Additional Information, which they do not have to provide to investors and potential investors, but which must be made available upon request at no additional charge. Specifically, the prospectus must include certain financial information such as net investment income, a reconciliation of net asset values, and portfolio turnover rate. The Statement of Additional Information includes the security's registration statement and annual reports, containing all of the condensed financial statements.

Communications with the public

NASD Rule 2210 Communications with the Public provides for the following definitions:
"Sales Literature" is any written or electronic communication, other than an advertisement, independently prepared reprint, institutional sales material, and correspondence, that is generally distributed or made generally available to customers or the public, including circulars, research reports, performance reports, or summaries, form letters, telemarketing scripts, seminar texts, reprints (that are not independently prepared reprints), or excerpts of any other advertisement, sales literature, or published article and press releases concerning a member's products or services.
"Correspondence" consists of any written letter or electronic mail message and any market letter distributed by a member to: (A) one or more of its existing retail customers, and (B) fewer than 25 prospective retail customers within any 30 calendar-day period.

Networking arrangements between members and financial institutions

Networking arrangements between members and financial institutions (FINRA Rule 3160) - a member that is a part of a networking agreement under which it conducts broker-dealer services on or off the premises of a financial institution is subject to the Rule.
Setting - the member is to be clearly identified and have its services distinguished from the services of the financial institution, have its name displayed where it conducts business, and maintain its services physically separate from that of the financial institution if at all possible.

Telemarketing

FINRA Rule 3230, which sets forth guidance on telemarketing activities, states that no member or person associated with a member shall initiate any outbound telephone call to:
Any person's residence before 8 a.m. or after 9 p.m., unless:
The member has an established business relationship with the person,
The member has received that person's prior express invitation or permission, or

- 23 -

The person called is a broker or dealer.
Any person that previously has stated that he or she does not wish to receive an outbound telephone call made by or on behalf of the member, or
Any person who has registered his or her telephone number on the Federal Trade Commission's national do-not-call registry.

The types of communications covered under FINRA Rule 3230 include:
   i.   Outbound calls from a member or associated person of a member to a non-broker dealer, including to wireless telephone numbers.
   ii. Outbound calls that have been outsourced to a third party.
   iii. Abandoned calls, which are those not answered by someone at the member within two seconds of the person's completed greeting.
   iv. Prerecorded messages.

For purposes of this rule, the term telemarketing is defined as consisting of or relating to a plan, program, or campaign involving at least one outbound telephone call, for example cold-calling. The term does not include the solicitation of sales through the mailing of written marketing materials, when the person making the solicitation does not solicit customers by telephone but only receives calls initiated by customers in response to the marketing materials and during those calls takes orders only without further solicitation.

Institutional account

Under FINRA Rule 4512, an institutional account is defined as the account of:
   1. A bank, savings and loan association, insurance company, or registered investment company
   2. An investment adviser registered either with the SEC under Section 203 of the Investment Advisers Act or with a state securities commission (or any agency or office performing like functions)
   3. Any other person (whether a natural person, corporation, partnership, trust, or otherwise) with total assets of at least $50 million

For these institutional accounts, or for purchases on securities on which no recommendation was made by the member, the member does not need to collect and retain the customer information relating to the customer's tax identification or Social Security number, occupation and name and address of employer, or status as an associated person with another member firm. Essentially, the only information that needs to be collected in these instances would be the appropriate names, responsibilities, authorizations, and signatures for anyone acting on behalf of the account.

Customer account information

FINRA Rule 4512 requires that for each new account that is opened, the following information must be collected and kept in the account's records:
1. Customer's name, address, and age
2. The names and responsibilities of any persons associated with the account other than the customer
3. Customer's signature, or the signature of an authorized representative in the case of an institutional customer
4. The names of any persons authorized to act on the customer's behalf
5. For accounts that are not institutional accounts, the member must also collect the customer's tax identification number or Social Security number, the occupation and name and address of the customer's employer and whether the customer is an associated person of another member firm.

All of this information is collected in order to protect both the member and the customer and to verify the identity of the customer to prevent illegal activity and unauthorized transactions.

Payments involving publications that influence the market price of a security

FINRA Rule 5230 states that no one may receive anything of value in exchange for publishing something that will influence the purchase or sale of a security. This includes any publications that occur via the Internet, television, and in writing. There are specific exemptions laid out in the rule, including the following:
A communication that is clearly an advertisement
A communication that includes a disclosure of the amount of compensation received
A research report, as specifically defined by NASD Rule 2711

Rule 482 of the Securities Act of 1933

In order to comply with Rule 482 of the Securities Act of 1933, any advertisement of an investment company must include a statement that advises an investor to consider the investment objectives, risks, and charges and expenses of the investment company carefully before investing; explains that the prospectus and, if available, the summary prospectus contain this and other information about the investment company; identifies a source from which an investor may obtain a prospectus and, if available, a summary prospectus; and states that the prospectus and, if available, the summary prospectus should be read carefully before investing. This disclosure is important because it ensures that each piece of investment company advertising will remind investors to carefully consider their investments and points them in the right direction to obtain additional information that is necessary to make an informed decision.

<u>Performance data</u>
In order to comply with Rule 482 of the Securities Act of 1933, any investment company advertisements including performance data must include the following:

i. A legend disclosing that the performance data quoted represents past performance; that past performance does not guarantee future results; that the investment return and principal value of an investment will fluctuate so that an investor's shares, when redeemed, may be worth more or less than their original cost; and that current performance may be lower or higher than the performance data quoted. The legend should also identify either a toll-free (or collect) telephone number or a Web site where an investor may obtain performance data current to the most recent month-end unless the advertisement includes total return quotations current to the most recent month ended seven business days prior to the date of use. An advertisement for a money market fund may omit the disclosure about principal value fluctuation; and

ii. If a sales load or any other nonrecurring fee is charged, the maximum amount of the load or fee, and if the sales load or fee is not reflected, a statement that the performance data does not reflect the deduction of the sales load or fee, and that, if reflected, the load or fee would reduce the performance quoted.

Sales literature deemed to be misleading

Rule 34b-1 provides important guidance for investment companies in developing sales literature that accurately portrays their security and would not be classified as misleading to investors. Specifically, sales literature must contain the following:
A statement that advises an investor to consider the investment objectives, risks and charges and expenses of the investment company carefully before investing, explains where the investor may obtain the prospectus and statement of additional information and that the prospectus should be read carefully before investing
Advertisements used prior to the effectiveness of the registration statement must include a "subject to completion" legend
Advertisements including performance data must include
A legend disclosing that data quoted represents past performance and that past performance does not guarantee future results
The investment return and principal value of an investment will fluctuate and the value may be worth more or less than the original investment
A toll-free phone line to obtain the most current performance data as of the most recent month-end
Maximum loads or fees that could be charged under the product.

Use of manipulative, deceptive, or other fraudulent devices

FINRA Rule 2020 Use of Manipulative, Deceptive or Other Fraudulent Devices states: "No member shall effect any transaction in, or induce the purchase or sale of, any security by means of any manipulative, deceptive, or other fraudulent device or contrivance." The importance of this rule is in ensuring the integrity of the capital markets and the confidence of retail investors that the markets are not "rigged" for the larger, institutional investors or those with critical inside information. A member would be in violation of Rule 2020 if he used falsified, enhanced financial reports to entice an investor to purchase a certain security. In addition to being dishonest and illegal, such activities have significantly negative repercussions for the markets as they reduce market efficiency and drastically reduce market participation among smaller investors if discovered.

Dealing with Non-members

NASD Rule 2420 states that members shall deal with non-members at the same prices, fees, and terms and commissions as in their dealings with the general public. Additionally, the rule states that no member shall:
In any transaction with any non-member broker or dealer, allow or grant to such non-member broker or dealer any selling concession, discount, or other allowance allowed by such member to a member of a registered securities association and not allowed to a member of the general public;
Join with any non-member broker or dealer in any syndicate or group contemplating the distribution to the public of any issue of securities or any part thereof; or
Sell any security to or buy any security from any non-member broker or dealer except at the same price at which at the time of such transaction such member would buy or sell such security, as the case may be, from or to a person who is a member of the general public not engaged in the investment banking or securities business.

Employment of manipulative and deceptive devices by brokers or dealers

Employment of manipulative and deceptive devices by brokers or dealers (Rule 10b-3) - it is prohibited for a broker or dealer to purchase or sell a security otherwise than on a national exchange with an act that is manipulative, deceptive, or fraudulent. The same is also prohibited for municipal securities dealers and municipal securities.
Employment of manipulative and deceptive devices (Rule 10b-5) - it is prohibited for any person to employ and device, scheme, or artifice to defraud; to make any untrue statements of material fact; or to engage in any act, practice, or course of business that would be a fraud or deceit upon any person in connections with the purchase or sale of any security.

Regulation D

Rule 501
Business combination - when two or more businesses come together under common control, such as in an acquisition.

Calculation of number of purchasers - provides exclusions when calculating total number of investors under a Regulation D offering, including family members, and accredited investors.

Executive officer - any president or vice president of a functional division of a company, or other policy making persons.

Issuer - any person who issues securities.

Purchaser representative - a person capable of making financial decisions and has a written agreement with the purchaser to represent them.

Rule 504

Rule 504 provides an exemption for companies to offer and sell up to $1 million of their securities in a 12-month period. To qualify for this exemption, the issuing company must not publicly advertise or solicit for these securities and the investors will receive restricted securities, which limit their ability to sell the securities in the secondary market. Rule 505 provides an exemption for companies to offer and sell up to $5 million of their securities in a 12-month period. To qualify for this exemption, the issuing company must not publicly advertise or solicit for these securities, the investors will receive restricted securities, and the issuing company can only sell to accredited investors or up to 35 other investors who do not meet the accredited investor requirements. Rule 506 allows many of the same exemptions available under Rule 505. However, under Rule 506 all non-accredited investors must be "sophisticated" investors. Once securities are sold under Rule 504, 505, or 506 of Regulation D, the issuing company must file a Form D, which contains the names and addresses of the company's owners and others involved in the promotion of the stock.

Form D

Form D is filed with the Securities and Exchange Commission when a company has issued securities under one of the exemptions provided under Rules 504, 505, and 506 of Regulation D. Generally speaking, these exemptions apply to small issuances of restricted securities to accredited or sophisticated investors. The information provided within Form D is limited to the names and addresses of the issuing company's owners and those other individuals involved in the promotion and distribution of the security being offered. While the Form D does not provide any financial information related to the issuing company or security, this information must be readily available and provided to investors upon request. Additionally, the financial information provided must not violate antifraud regulations.

Accredited investor and other excluded investors

The five classifications of an accredited investor are as follows:
  i.   a bank
  ii. an insurance company
  iii. an investment company registered under the Investment Company Act of 1940
  iv. a Small Business Investment Company licensed by the Small Business Administration

v.   an employee benefit plan or individual retirement account which is subject to the Employee Retirement Income Security Act of 1974 (ERISA) and in which the investment decision is made by a fiduciary

Besides accredited investors, the other three classifications of investors that are excluded from the calculation of number of purchasers under Rules 505 and 506 of Regulation D are as follows:
1. a natural person with net worth, excluding primary residence, in excess of $1 million
2. a natural person with individual income of $200,000 in each of the past 2 years, or $300,000 income jointly with their spouse
3. a trust, corporation, charitable organization, or partnership with assets in excess of $5 million

Rule 135a of the Securities Act of 1933

Under Rule 135a of the Securities Act of 1933, generic advertising will not be considered as an offering of a security so long as it meets at least one of the following requirements:
i.   Explanatory information relating to securities of investment companies generally or to the nature of investment companies, or to services offered in connection with the ownership of such securities,
ii.   The mention or explanation of investment companies of different generic types or having various investment objectives, such as balanced funds, growth funds, income funds, leveraged funds, specialty funds, variable annuities, bond funds, and no-load funds,
iii. Offers, descriptions, and explanation of various products and services not constituting a security subject to registration under the act, provided that such offers, descriptions, and explanations do not relate directly to the desirability of owning or purchasing a security issued by a registered investment company,
iv.   Invitation to inquire for further information,

Email blast
An email blast that is sent to thousands of recipients and contains only a description of a firm's services and their general investment strategy would constitute generic advertising as it would fall under at least one of the four categories provided in Rule 135a of the Securities Act of 1933. More specifically, this email blast would constitute generic advertising because it is only generally describing the services and investment strategy of the investment company and is not specifically naming any particular securities or offerings. Under the provisions of Rule 135a, generic advertising does not need to be preceded or accompanied by a prospectus, since they do not contain specific information relating to a particular fund or any performance information.

Evaluate Customers' Financial Information, Identify Investment Objectives, Provide Information on Investment Products, and Make Suitable Recommendations

Determining a suitable investment recommendation

Age, marital status, and dependents

An investor's age is critical in determining a suitable investment recommendation because younger investors typically have much longer time horizons and are therefore able to take more substantial risks in order to achieve their goals. Also, as younger investors continue to save and invest the impact of dollar cost averaging can help achieve attractive returns through all market cycles. Older investors, to the contrary, typically have shorter time horizons as they near retirement or other significant life events and are more concerned with the protection of principal as their level of retirement income has already been largely determined. Whether an investor is married and has dependents also plays a critical role in determining a suitable investment recommendation as a single investor is able to take greater risks and will typically have more disposable income, or ability to take risks. A married investor with five children, however, will have more of his income committed to providing for his family and will likely have several near-term life events to save for including higher education and marriages. This investor will have to consider not only how his investments will impact him but also how they will impact his ability to provide for his family.

Income, expenses, disposable income, and discretionary income

Income is important in determining a suitable investment recommendation because investors with greater income typically have a greater ability to take risk, all else being equal, than investors with less income. However, investors with greater income may be able to meet their investment and income objectives with a lower return and less risk than investors with less income who may need to achieve a higher rate of return on a smaller base of investment principal. Additionally, investors in different areas with similar incomes may have very different discretionary incomes, defined as after-tax income. Investors who lose more of their income to taxes will have less to invest. Income is just one side of the equation when making a suitable investment recommendation, as a good adviser must also consider that investor's expenses. Two investors with the same income may have significantly different amounts of disposable income, defined as after-tax income less expenses. Thus, the amount of income, expenses, and taxes all play into the amount of discretionary income an investor has to choose how much from which to invest.

Assets and liabilities, liquid assets, and insurance needs

An investor's personal balance sheet, or his assets and liabilities at any given point in time, is critically important in helping an adviser determine a suitable investment recommendation. An investor's other assets may include real estate, bank accounts, other brokerage accounts, and retirement plans, while common personal liabilities include mortgages, auto loans, and credit cards. The stronger an investor's personal balance sheet (excess of assets over liabilities), the better positioned that investor will be to invest a greater portion of his funds and to take a greater level of risk for his investments.

Additionally, the proportion of that investor's assets that are liquid will play a role in helping an investment adviser determine the appropriate amount and type of investments to recommend. An investor with a greater proportion of liquid assets can utilize those assets to meet current obligations, compared to an investor with most illiquid assets such as real estate where the investment account would be the first source of funds to meet current liabilities. Finally, an investor's need for insurance, which is driven by the amount of current and future liabilities, will reduce the amount of discretionary income available for investments as a portion of that income will be directed toward the insurance purchase.

Participation in retirement programs, participation in benefit plans, and tax status

An investor's active participation in retirement programs will increase his ability to take risk with his remaining investment portfolio because his ability to fund his retirement lifestyle will not be as severely impacted by gains or losses in his personal portfolio as an investor with a lower level of participation in a retirement program. The safety net of the retirement plan participation will allow the investor to take additional risks in his personal portfolio. Additionally, an investor with stronger benefit plans will not have as many out-of-pocket expenses to be concerned with as an investor with a weaker benefit plan offering. Thus, the former can choose to redirect a greater portion of his income to his personal investment portfolio instead of his other obligations. Finally, an investor's tax status will help an adviser determine both the appropriate amount and type of investments to recommend. All else being equal, an investor in a lower tax rate can earn a higher after-tax rate of return than an investor in a higher tax rate. Thus, a lower tax rate investor may not see as significant a benefit from tax-exempt bonds or other asset classes with preferred tax treatment.

Example scenario

> A single man, age 60, plans on retiring at age 62. He holds significant liquid assets, has a high discretionary income, and maintains large balances in his corporate retirement plans. What additional information would you need to know in order to make a suitable investment recommendation?

Based on only the information provided above, it appears this investor could take a relatively aggressive approach to his personal investing. However, without additional information it could be difficult to make a proper recommendation. For instance, a good adviser would want to confirm the investor's tax status. It's likely that this investor is a high tax payer; thus, the adviser may want to consider a tax-preferred investment such as municipal bonds. Additionally, although we know this investor has a high level of discretionary income at the current time, we don't know if he has a significant number of dependents, which may change that discretionary income at some time in the near future. For instance, this investor could have triplets about to enter a private university, completely changing his discretionary income in the coming years.

<u>Example scenario</u>
> *Your client provides you with the following personal information: age 25, male, single, income of $74,000 per year, expenses of $26,000 per year. Which piece of information is irrelevant to your recommendation and why? What additional information would you want to know in order to ensure you make a suitable recommendation?*

Based on the information provided about this investor, the only piece of information that is not useful for an adviser is that the investor is male. Age, marital status, income, and expenses are all necessary to assist an adviser in providing a suitable recommendation. Gender, however, has no bearing on an adviser's recommendation. Although age, marital status, income, and expenses are all useful in determining a recommendation, an adviser would need additional information in order to ensure he is making a suitable recommendation. For instance, an adviser would want to know the status of this investor's current balance sheet (assets and liabilities) as well as the amount of his liquid assets. For many investors this age, student loans represent a significant portion of the liability and can play an important role in determining investment objectives.

Investment objectives

<u>Preservation of capital</u>
Aptly named, the goal of a preservation of capital investment objective is to preserve the initial capital investment (i.e., minimize the risk of an investment loss). To achieve this objective, an investor must be willing to sacrifice much of the upside potential of investment return in order to minimize the risk of a negative return. This trade-off fits within the concept of the risk/return framework, as the investor must give up higher return potential in favor or reduced volatility. Perhaps the best example of a security that would achieve this preservation of capital objective is a treasury bill or treasury bond, in which the principal investment (the face value of the bond) is guaranteed by the U.S. government. Other securities that are considered to be highly secure are those issued by government agencies such as Fannie Mae and Freddie Mac, which also offer a slightly higher return than treasury securities as the principal does not have the same level of security and guarantee.

Current income

The goal of a current income investment objective is to provide a source of current income. The current income investment objective is typically utilized by investors who have a shorter time horizon or who may be looking to their investment portfolio to supplement their current income. Additionally, investors employing this strategy typically are looking to this income that is generated by the investment to fund current obligations and thus look to a minimum level of volatility as their obligations are typically more fixed in nature. If an investor did not have a need for this current income, he would be more likely to seek an investment with a different objective as current income exposes the investor to reinvestment risk, which can generate losses in markets with falling rates. Corporate bonds are a common example of a security that provides current income through semiannual coupon payments. Additionally, large, stable equity securities can also provide current income through relatively predictable and stable dividend payments. These equity securities, however, typically provide a lower level of current income than fixed income securities and expose the investor to a greater degree of principal risk.

Capital appreciation

Contrary to a current income investment objective, a capital appreciation investment objective seeks to achieve a high level of return through growth in the price of the security. As a result, investors with this objective would prefer that funds be reinvested into the high growth company instead of being paid out in the form of dividends. Investors pursuing this investment objective typically have longer time horizons as capital appreciation is considered to be a much riskier source of return than current income or capital preservation. Equity securities, particularly those of small and mid-cap companies, are a great example of the capital appreciation investment objective as they typically reinvest their earnings and pay out very low, if any, dividends. However, these securities are also considered riskier as they are less stable and business conditions and performance can fluctuate much more wildly and success can hinge on the success or failure of a single product.

Growth and income

The goal of a growth and income investment objective is to achieve investment returns through a combination of both current income and capital appreciation. This investment objective lies on the spectrum between the options of achieving returns through current income only (corporate bonds) and by capital appreciation only (small-cap equity securities). Additionally, this growth and income investment objective is a moderate risk objective as the current income portion of the portfolio mitigates some of the risk that results from the capital appreciation portion of the investment portfolio. One example of a growth and income investment objective is a large cap equity security that pays a consistent dividend. In this example, an investor would receive current income through dividends and would see capital appreciation through changes in the price of the equity security.

Aggressive growth

The goal of an aggressive growth investment objective is to achieve a very high level rate of return through capital appreciation. This investment objective is a specific subset of the capital appreciation objective in which the securities that are targeted include only those with extremely high expected rates of return. In order to achieve those rates of return, investors with this aggressive growth investment objective must be willing to undergo a higher level of volatility and risk. As such, investors with this objective typically have a much longer time horizon in order to minimize the impacts of market downturns. One example of this aggressive growth investment objective is a small-cap equity security, which does not pay dividends and which is expected to provide annual returns of somewhere in the range of 15%. However, this security may have large swings in returns and the standard deviation likely exceeds 30%.

Tax exempt income

The goal of a tax-exempt income investment objective is similar to that of a current income investment objective, with the primary difference being the desire to have the current income be tax exempt. Although tax-exempt bonds typically provide for lower coupon rates than taxable bonds, investors must calculate the taxable equivalent yield, defined as the yield divided by 1 minus the investor's tax rate, so that the yield can be appropriately compared to taxable bonds. Some investors may prefer to earn tax-exempt income if they pay particularly high rates or if they feel that the tax-equivalent yield on tax-exempt bonds provides a more attractive risk-adjusted return than yields on taxable bonds. One example of a security for a tax exempt income investment objective is a municipal bond, which is exempt from federal taxes and, possibly, many state and local taxes as well.

Defensive investment strategy

A defensive investment strategy is one in which an investor is primarily concerned with protection of investment principal rather than potential gains. Put into the context of the trade-off between risk and return, an investor utilizing a defensive strategy would be primarily concerned with mitigating risk and would try to maximize expected returns given an acceptable level of risk. Typically, a defensive investment strategy would be utilized by investors who are either older or would have a shorter investing time horizon. Contrary to younger investors, older investors or those saving for a near-term event do not have sufficient time to wait through market fluctuations. For instance, a 60-year-old investor plans to retire at age 62 and will need to start drawing from his investment principal in 2 years. In order to ensure he has sufficient savings to last through retirement, he is likely to utilize a defensive investment strategy. If he were to suffer significant losses in value and then had to start drawing down those assets, his ability to fund his retirement would be substantially hindered.

Aggressive investment strategy

An aggressive investment strategy is one in which an investor is primarily concerned with achieving a certain level of return and is willing to accept a higher than normal level of risk in order to achieve that return. Typical investments within an aggressive investment strategy may include small and mid-cap equity securities and international securities, all of which have potential for higher returns but also substantially higher levels of risk. As such, investors choosing to invest in aggressive strategies typically have longer time horizons so that market fluctuations should have time to correct prior to the point at which they will need to liquidate or begin drawing down funds. Younger investors who are saving for a retirement that is 30 or 40 years in the future will likely pursue an aggressive investment strategy. Additionally, investors who need to achieve a high level of return may choose to pursue an aggressive strategy. However, even investors choosing an aggressive strategy should seek to minimize risk at a given level of expected return through proper diversification and asset allocation techniques.

Financial status, investment objectives, and risk tolerance of clients

In order to provide suitable investment recommendations for clients, advisers must conduct thorough due diligence to learn about their client's financial status, investment objectives, and risk tolerance. Just because an investor believes he will achieve a 20% return by investing in ultra-aggressive Fund A does not mean it is a suitable investment for that investor and only by knowing detailed information about that client and what he is looking to achieve can the adviser properly make recommendations and help the client weigh the risks of each investment alternative. It is up to the adviser to help individual investors see past the numerous behavioral biases that tend to influence the investment decision-making process and to objectively weigh the relative merits of each investment alternative to make the optimal decision to achieve their goals.

Impact on risk tolerance

Short-term liquidity needs

Short term liquidity needs impact an investor's risk tolerance because an investor's ability to take risk is inversely correlated to an investor's short-term liquidity needs. As an investor's short-term liquidity needs increase, his ability to take risk in his investment portfolio decreases because he will want to ensure that he is not drawing down his pool of invested assets during a downward swing in performance that could significantly impact his long-term performance. Withdrawing funds from an investment portfolio at a low valuation before assets have had a chance to rebound will significantly hinder long-term performance because fewer assets will remain invested to experience the upside return. One security that may not be suitable is a small-cap equity security, because the wide fluctuations in the price of the security will make it difficult to appropriately time your withdrawals of invested assets.

- 35 -

Long-term liquidity needs

Long-term liquidity needs provide for much more flexibility in risk tolerance than do short-term liquidity needs. While short-term liquidity needs make it more difficult to appropriately time withdrawals so that withdrawals are not taken at times of low performance, with a longer time horizon until liquidity is needed, an investor can increase the risk in his portfolio without being adversely impacted by the fluctuations in portfolio value. With longer term liquidity needs, an investor has more time to experience the fluctuations in the price of a security without having immediate needs to withdraw those funds. Thus, the investor can choose an ideal time to diversify out of the riskier assets and into a safer portfolio as he approaches his future liquidity needs. This investor will want to ensure that he invests in securities that provide enough expected return to meet his financial objectives. Thus, a more conservative investment may not be suitable for an investor with long term liquidity needs.

Significant increase in an investor's income level

A significant increase in an investor's income will, all other factors remaining constant, increase an investor's risk tolerance because his discretionary income will have also increased. However, it would be important for an adviser to also take into consideration how that increase in income is likely to influence the investor's future expenses and tax rates. Along with that increased income, the investor will most likely also increase expenses proportionately. Thus, although he has greater income, he may not have any additional discretionary income. Additionally, he will also be paying higher taxes as his income increases, so he will not have experienced the same proportionate increase in his disposable income as the increase in his total income. Finally, the investor's marital status and number of dependents is likely to impact how that increase in income may be translated into an increase in expenses. With a wife and several children, it's more likely that the investor will increase expenses more so than for a single investor with no children.

Significant increase in inflation

An increase in inflation essentially works as a reduction in an investor's expected real rate of return. For instance, assume that an investor's portfolio is expected to return a nominal rate of 7% and inflation is 2%; thus, his expected real return is 5%. Now consider the situation in which the inflation rate rises to 4%. His expected real return has now fallen to 3%, but he is still subject to the same level of risk. The investor must consider whether he is willing to take additional risk in order to increase his nominal return to 9% and restore his expected real return. Alternatively, the investor may decide that he is not willing to accept any additional risk and must reconsider his financial objectives under the assumption of a 3% real return.

Willingness to take risk and ability to take risk

An investor's willingness to take risk is a behavioral trait that is not related to an investor's personal financial situation. It is driven by each investor's personal preferences and willingness to accept and live with volatility. On the other hand, an investor's ability to take risk is driven by an investor's financial situation and objectives. For instance, a 60-year-old investor who is retiring within five years may have a risk-taking personality and a strong desire to "beat the market" and "pick winners" in the stock market. However, that investor must also consider his financial objectives and, specifically, his short-term time horizon until his retirement when deciding upon an appropriate investment objective. Advisers must consider both an investor's willingness and ability to take risk when making an investment recommendation. The final recommendation should typically be based on whichever factor results in a more conservative approach, as an adviser would never want to make a recommendation with which the investor was uncomfortable or which would jeopardize that investor's financial objectives.

Standards of Commercial Honor and Principles of Trade

FINRA Rule 2010 Standards of Commercial Honor and Principles of Trade states that "a member, in the conduct of its business, shall observe high standards of commercial honor and just and equitable principles of trade." Broadly speaking, this rule encourages members to be just and equitable in their dealings, although no real specific guidance is provided. One example of a violation of this rule would be a member who treats different customers differently based upon their gender, ethnicity, religion, or other personal attributes. This biased approach to customers violates the just and equitable charge of Rule 2010, as well as a number of other FINRA rules, and would result in significant repercussions for the member. A member must treat each customer equitably, considering each customer's individual circumstances and investment objectives.

Know Your Customer

FINRA Rule 2090 Know Your Customer requires advisers to use "reasonable diligence" when opening and servicing customer accounts. Part of this reasonable diligence is knowing the "essential facts" about every customer, including those required to (i) effectively service the account, (ii) act in accordance with special handling instructions for the account, (iii) understand the authority of each person acting on behalf of the account and (iv) comply with applicable laws, regulations, and rules. The importance of this rule in is ensuring that each investor's account is handled in accordance with the investor's wishes and in accordance with all rules and laws. This provides peace of mind to the investor that his account is being maintained and serviced properly not only at the account opening, but throughout the entire length of the relationship that the investor maintains with that adviser.

<u>Essential facts concerning every customer</u>
The four "essential facts" contemplated in FINRA Rule 2090-Know Your Customer are those required to (i) effectively service the customer's account, (ii) act in accordance with any special handling instructions for the account, (iii) understand the authority of each person acting on behalf of the customer, and (iv) comply with applicable laws, regulations, and rules. These essential facts are important because they help provide peace of mind to investors that their accounts are being handled in accordance with their requests. Additionally, they can be assured that only those individuals with proper authority to act on behalf of their account will be allowed to do so and that the account will be operated in accordance with all of the applicable rules and regulations. This responsibility lies with the broker or adviser, who are the experts in these rules and regulations, and not with the individual investor, who likely is not familiar with these rules or does not have time to constantly monitor and ensure compliance.

Suitability

FINRA Rule 2111-Suitability states that an adviser must have a reasonable basis to believe that the investment(s) he is recommending is suitable for the investor based upon the information collected during the due diligence process including age, other investments, financial objectives, tax status, investment experience, time horizon, liquidity needs, and risk tolerance. This reasonable basis for an investment recommendation is critically important in helping protect investors from making investments that may not be suitable for their financial situation. Specifically, investors may often be lured into investments with potentially attractive returns, but with correspondingly great risks. While investments like these may be suitable for investors with significant other wealth and assets or experienced investors, this would not be a suitable recommendation for a new investor whose investment represents a significant portion of his personal assets. Additionally, this rule puts much of the responsibility for determining a suitable investment onto the adviser, who must educate his client on the risks and potential benefits of each investment alternative under consideration.

The new FINRA Rule 2111 expands upon the previous NASD Rule 2310 by specifying the factors to be considered in developing the investment profile, including an investor's age, other investments, financial situation and needs, tax status, investment objectives, investment experience, investment time horizon, liquidity needs, risk tolerance, and any other information disclosed by the investor. This is an important expansion because the delineation of these factors provides more clarity for advisers on the most important factors that need to be considered for each investor to which they make a recommendation.

The new Rule 2111 also provides that, while the rule applies to all recommended investment strategies and the term strategy is meant to be applied broadly, the rule does not cover general educational materials that firms may produce, as FINRA believes this educational material to be important to creating an educated investing public. This educational material is exempt from the rule so long as it does not include any specific recommendations of particular securities.

The new factors added to FINRA Rule 2111 include an investor's age, investment experience, time horizon, liquidity needs, and risk tolerance. An investor's age and time horizon are typically closely linked and both are important in determining suitability because a younger investor will typically have a longer time horizon than an older investor, and will thus be able to take more risk than an older investor with a shorter time horizon.

An investor's investment experience will help the adviser in determining whether a more complex investment may be appropriate. An investor with more experience is likely more familiar with investment analysis and more likely to understand complex risks, while a novice investor may require more education from the adviser prior to making any recommendations. Liquidity needs are also important in determining a suitable recommendation in terms of both the timing and magnitude of the liquidity requirement. An investor with near term liquidity needs or a larger liquidity need must ensure that any investments can be quickly converted to cash to meet current obligations. To minimize losses and optimize performance, these investments should typically be much less risky in nature because of their short time horizon. Finally, an investor's risk tolerance must also be considered as the adviser will want to ensure that the investor understands and is comfortable with the level of risk in his portfolio.

Fixed and variable annuities

<u>Payments to the annuitant, guarantees, risks, and contract holder objectives</u>
One of the primary differences between fixed and variable annuities, and the most notable to policy owners, is that a fixed annuity provides for a guaranteed, level payment, while a variable annuity's payment will fluctuate based upon the performance of underlying subaccount investments. The fixed annuity will provide the investor with certain guarantees as to minimum rates and charges, so that an investor can plan a minimum benefit distribution. A variable annuity, however, is only guaranteed with respect to maximum charges. It does not, however, provide any type of guarantee of investment performance, since that is controlled by the investor and a function of the investment allocation he adopts. Without the investment performance guarantees, the variable annuity is significantly riskier than a fixed annuity and is better suited for an investor with a longer time horizon or flexible liquidity needs so as to manage peaks and troughs in performance.

<u>Types of variable annuities</u>
An immediate variable annuity is one in which the initial contribution into the annuity is converted into annuitization units, which then increase or decrease in value depending upon the investment performance of underlying subaccount allocations and payments begin to occur immediately. In a deferred annuity, however, the initial contribution is converted into accumulation units, which are not

paid out until some specified period of time and continue to increase or decrease in value, depending upon investment performance.

Single pay annuities are funded with one initial payment at the time of issue. Single pay annuities can be either immediate or deferred annuities. Periodic payment annuities are funded over a series of periodic payments and could only be utilized within a deferred annuity.

Features of variable annuity contracts

The four key features of a variable annuity contract are tax-deferred accumulation, ownership interests, voting rights, and distribution options. Contract values within a variable annuity contract grow on a tax-deferred basis, meaning that more funds remain invested to reap the benefits of compound interest right up until such time as it is paid out. Annuities are typically owned by the individual expecting to receive the ultimate benefit payments, but a beneficiary must also be maintained on file so that, in the event of a death of a contract holder, the proceeds can be paid to the proper individuals. A variable annuity contract holder has similar voting rights to a variable life insurance policyholder, in that the contract holder can vote to elect the board of directors of the issuing company. Finally, variable annuities offer a number of distribution options, ranging from payments in a lump-sum or over a specified number of years or even a life annuity, which provides for the payment of benefits over the remaining life of the contract holder.

Contractual provisions: Variable annuities provide a mortality guarantee, which specifies a minimum death benefit that will be paid to the investor's beneficiary if he should die before he begins receiving payments from the contract. Additionally, a variable annuity also specifies the maximum charges that the issuing company can impose within the contract. These minimum guaranteed expenses are important for investors to consider given the long-term nature of investments in variable annuities. Variable annuities provide for a death benefit that is payable to the contract holder's beneficiary before he begins receiving the benefit distributions. As mentioned above, the death benefit will be guaranteed to be at or equal to a given level, but may also be higher depending on the investment performance of the contract. Finally, a variable annuity also has a surrender value equal to the contributions into the contract plus investment earnings less expenses and charges. This surrender value, which may be impacted by enhancements or surrender charges, is the amount that the investor would receive upon a surrender of the contract. Any gains over cost basis would be taxable to the contract holder.

Under Section 1035 of the Internal Revenue Code, variable annuities can be exchanged tax-free for another variable annuity contract. This is an important provision that allows investors who may have a significant amount of taxable gain over cost basis to move into a newer policy with lower charges, if available. Many variable annuity contracts, in an effort to improve performance in early years and to entice investors to keep their contracts for at least a given period of time, will apply either enhancements or surrender charges to the value of the contract. This amount

- 40 -

is only received upon surrender and typically is not allocated among the variable subaccount options. Dollar cost averaging is one way for contract holders in a variable annuity contract to ensure that they invest similar amounts in both up and down markets, which means that more units are purchased in down markets and fewer units in up markets. This provision is only relevant for periodic payment annuities.

Many variable annuity contracts will contain a level sales charge that is applied to deposits into the contract. This sales charge is used to compensate the broker who sold the contract and to cover the costs associated with issuing the contract. The maximum amount of this sales charge must be specified in the contract. A contingent deferred sales charge may impact the amount that a contract holder would receive upon surrender. For instance, an investor may be able to pay a lower level sales charge by purchasing a policy with a larger contingent deferred sales charge, which is only applied in the case of a surrender within a given period of time. Thus, this provision encourages contract holders to maintain their contracts. For variable annuities, the underlying investment options are managed by investment advisers, who charge investment management fees for their services. These fees are netted out of the performance of the underlying subaccounts that are selected.

As with a variable life insurance policy, a contract holder must pay certain state and federal taxes upon deposits into a variable annuity contract. The premium taxes may vary by state and the DAC taxes will vary by issuing company and the assumptions used to amortize this cost. Mortality and expense risk charges are explicit charges each month within the contract that seek to compensate the issuing company for taking on the risk that the contract holder will pass away. Since the death benefits are greater than contract values, the possibility of the death of a contract holder represents a financial risk to the issuing company. Finally, administrative expenses are also taken from contract values on a periodic basis to compensate the issuing company for the costs of providing reporting, projections, billings, and other administrative functions. These charges are typically minimal in relation to overall policy values.

Growth in value of accumulation units, withdrawal of annuitization units, and conversion of accumulation units to annuitization

Throughout the accumulation phase, which is the period in which contributions are made into the variable annuity contract and prior to the beginning of benefit distributions, deposits are allocated into a variety of investment options and grow in accordance with the performance of that asset allocation, less reductions for expenses, and fees.

Once the contract is annuitized, at the beginning of the payment stream, the accumulation units that have been growing throughout the accumulation phase are converted into annuitization units. The rate of conversion of accumulation units into annuitization units will be spelled out in the contract and will take into account a number of factors, including actuarial life expectancy and the assumed interest rate. Whether or not the payments rise or fall in value depends upon the relative performance of the subaccount investments in relation to the assumed interest rate.

Variable life insurance

A variable universal life insurance policy allows policyholders the same premium and death benefit flexibility as with a universal life insurance policy. The primary difference is in the crediting of cash values, which in a variable life insurance policy is based on a menu of available fund managers and asset classes and styles. Variable universal life insurance policies are particularly attractive to investors who utilize insurance as a way to achieve tax-deferred growth of assets. Additionally, with exceptional investment performance, the policyholder can also end up receiving a higher death benefit as insurance laws mandate ratios between cash values and death benefits for given age/gender combinations. Along with this increased reward comes increased risk. In addition to the cost of insurance charges, a policyholder is also subject to investment losses that can result in additional premium payments or lowered coverage amounts.

Voting rights of policyholders

Similar to an open-end investment company, or mutual fund, a policyholder of a variable life insurance contract is entitled to voting rights in determining the life insurance company's board of directors. The voting rights of a policyholder differ from those of a mutual fund, however, in that a policyholder does not have the authority to vote on the investment operations or investment management of the insurance company's general account or any of the separate accounts. Voting for the insurance company's board of directors is typically conducted during the company's annual meeting of shareholders or policyholders, depending upon whether the life insurance company is a for-profit corporation with shareholders or a mutual insurer with only policyholders.

Contractual provisions

Many life insurance contracts, especially term and group life insurance contracts, offer a conversion privilege, which allows the policyholder to convert the group or individual term policy into individually owned, permanent insurance without further medical underwriting.

All variable life insurance policies, which provide for explicit charges related to sales loads, insurance risk charges, and cost of insurance charges, must set forth the maximum charges that can be assessed within the contract. This provides an important guarantee to investors and allows them to consider not only the current charges, but what charges the insurer could impose in future policy years. Variable life insurance policies, provided that there is a remaining cash value, cannot be terminated at the election of the insurance company. The policyholder does maintain the right to surrender the policy at any time, although any gains above what was paid into the policy will be taxable upon surrender. The surrender value is the total value of each of the underlying subaccounts within a variable life insurance policy. This is the amount, prior to any enhancements or surrender charges that would be received by the policyholder upon surrender.

Dollar cost averaging

Many variable life insurance policies provide for dollar cost averaging, in which a policyholder contributes the same dollar amount to each of the underlying subaccounts over a period of time. The benefit to investors is that by investing a consistent dollar amount, more underlying units of the subaccount are purchased when the price of the subaccount is depressed and fewer units are purchased when the value is higher. Thus, this is an easy way for policyholders to ensure that they are not "chasing the market," a common mistake among retail investors that typically leads to a greater amount purchased at higher prices and too little investment when values are temporarily depressed. It's important to keep in mind that the investor should not be investing in funds that do not have strong future prospects, regardless of how depressed the subaccount value may be relative to prior purchases.

Sales charge structure

Life insurance companies typically deduct both a sales charge and a premium expense charge from contributions to a variable life insurance policy. The sales charge is used to compensate the broker who sold the policy and also to cover the costs of issuing the policy. The sales charge is limited by the maximums set forth in the policy contract, typically in the range of 3 to 5%. Additionally, the insurance company deducts a portion of the premium deposits in order to cover certain state premium and DAC (Deferred Acquisition Cost) taxes. Premium tax rates vary by state and are assessed directly against the policy cash value. Different carriers treat the collection of DAC taxes differently, as that tax is due by the insurance company and just collected, typically over time, from the insurance contract.

Charges in a contract

When a policyholder purchases a variable life insurance policy from an insurance company, the contract is priced in large part based upon expected mortality across the insurer's book of business. Mortality costs are policy charges imposed against a policy's cash value to compensate the insurer for taking the risk that mortality may occur sooner than projected.

Each of the subaccounts within a variable life insurance policy has operating expenses similar to those within a mutual fund. These are the costs of the investment adviser, operating the fund, custodial fees, etc., and are assessed against the returns that are credited to the account. Insurance carriers also charge an administrative expense within variable life insurance contracts for the work done in reporting policy values, tracking billings, coordinating subaccount valuations, and a wide variety of other administrative tasks that require significant resources. Cost of insurance charges are assessed each month against the cash value of the policy in an amount equal to the expected mortality of the insured multiplied by the net amount at risk (the difference between the death benefit and cash value).

<u>Settlement options</u>
The policyholder of a variable life insurance policy has a number of settlement options. The most common eventual settlement of a variable life insurance policy is through the death of the insured. In this instance, the death benefits specified by the policy are payable tax-free to the policyholder's beneficiary(ies). Another alternative for the policy owner is to surrender the policy. With a surrender, the policyholder receives an amount equivalent to the cash value of the policy, adjusted for any enhancements or surrender charges, and forfeits all rights to any future death benefits from the policy. It is important to note that any amount surrendered that exceeds the cost basis, or the amount invested, in the contract will be taxable to the policyholder. Finally, the policyholder can elect to exchange the policy for another insurance policy or for a variable annuity. This can be accomplished, tax-free, under Section 1035 of the Internal Revenue Code, frequently referred to as a "1035 Exchange."

<u>Cash value</u>
Upon the issuance of a variable life insurance policy, the premium deposit is charged with any applicable sales loads and premium expenses and is allocated in the subaccounts specified by the policyholder. The cash value of the policy will grow based upon the performance of the selected subaccount(s), less any mortality charges, investment management fees, administrative expenses, and cost of insurance charges, which are all typically applied monthly or quarterly. In order to maintain its qualification as insurance, a variable life insurance policy must maintain a certain ratio between the amount of the cash value and the death benefit. This ratio is determined based on the issuing carrier's mortality tables factoring in age and gender. As the cash value increases over time with strong investment performance, the death benefit rises accordingly.

Whole life insurance

A whole life insurance policy requires a fixed premium payment over a given period of time (i.e., 10 years or through age 90) and in return provides for a level death benefit over the life of the contract. The cash value of the contract increases according to a rate specified in the contract at the time of issue and the insurance company, not the insured, is at risk of investing the assets in such a way as to make a profitable return on the funds. The insured who purchases a whole life policy is truly seeking the protection offered by the death benefit of the policy, as opposed to one who purchases a universal life or variable universal life insurance policy and may be more interested in tax-deferred accumulation of assets.

Universal life insurance

A universal life policy differs from a whole life policy primarily through the flexibility of premium payments. Additionally, any amount paid into the policy as premium is credited with interest based upon a rate set by the insurer and also is debited with cost of insurance charges based upon the insured's demographic information and the amount of net amount at risk (excess of death benefit over cash value). The death benefits can be much higher for a given level of premium than in a whole life contract, but the charges taken from policy values will be higher. The risk to a policyholder is that rates will decline and additional premium payments will be required to keep the policy from lapsing. A universal life insurance purchaser falls in the middle of the insurance risk spectrum, retaining exposure to cash value growth through the crediting rate and keeping premium flexibility, but also taking on the additional risk that comes with a lower guaranteed performance.

Taking a loan from a life insurance policy

Life insurance policies typically contain provisions that allow the policyholder to take a loan against the policy up to a certain percentage of the policy's cash value (often 90%). The life insurance policy will specify the amount of the interest that will accrue on the loan balance, which will be due at the next policy anniversary. Additionally, the policy will specify a rate of interest to be credited on the borrowed cash value that will be some spread below the loan interest rate. Thus, policy loans are oftentimes an efficient source of borrowing because of the minimal loan spreads in most products and because the loan is tax-free to the policyholder. If a policy lapses while there is a loan outstanding, then the amount of the loan immediately becomes taxable income to the policyholder. However, if the policyholder dies while a loan is outstanding, the loan is repaid through a portion of the proceeds and the beneficiary simply receives the death benefit net of the outstanding loan. This does not impact the taxability of either the death proceeds or the loaned amount.

Risks with purchasing domestic corporate bonds

An investor purchasing domestic corporate bonds will face a number of risks. Two of the most important of these risks include interest rate risk and reinvestment risk. The interest rate risk in this circumstance arises from the fact that the investor would be subject to a reduction in the value of the security if market interest rates rise. Additionally, the investor would be subject to reinvestment risk if market interest rates fall as their receipt of coupon payments could not be reinvested at previously prevailing rates. This assumption that coupon payments can be reinvested at the same rate is one principal assumption underlying the calculation of the yield to maturity of a fixed income security, a common measure of fixed income yield.

Risk with purchasing an emerging markets equity mutual fund

An investor purchasing an emerging markets equity security will face a number of risks. Two of the most important of these risks include social and political risk and currency exchange risk. Due to the less stable nature of many governments within emerging markets, emerging markets equities typically require a higher level of expected returns to compensate investors for the additional level of risk to the security. The real risk of political instability is that changes in the government structure or in the government's attitude toward business and international integration could negatively impact the price of a security. This risk has nothing to do with the business itself, only the country and political environment in which it operates. Emerging markets equity securities are also subject to currency exchange risk as unexpected changes in exchange rates can decrease some or all of an investment's gains.

Risks with purchasing a market neutral hedge fund that is priced monthly

An investor purchasing a market neutral hedge fund will face a number of risks. Two of the most important of these risks include liquidity risk and business risk. With any security that is priced monthly, it can be difficult for investors to adequately liquidate their position if there are substantial changes in either the position of the fund or if the investor's personal situation changes such that liquidity is required. Additionally, with a liquidity restriction it may be more likely that multiple investors will choose to exit the fund at the same time, thus driving down the price each investor will receive for their share of the security. Additionally, with a market neutral hedge fund the fund manager will be trying to pick individual securities across the market such that the fund's gains or losses are attributable to the securities chosen and not to any assumptions about broad market performance.

Risk with purchasing an equity security in a multinational conglomerate

An investor purchasing an equity security in a multinational conglomerate will face a number of risks. Two of the most important of these risks include currency exchange risk and business risk. Currency exchange risk will play a role in determining the required return for this security because all revenue derived from foreign operations will be subject to translation before inclusion in the financial statements, which are denominated in the home currency. Depending upon the countries in which the company operates and the expected currency exchange risk for those countries against the home currency, investors may require an additional expected return. Additionally, the investor will be subject to business risk. Any unexpected downward shifts in the financial performance, or projected financial performance, of the company will result in a reduction in the value of the equity security.

Risk with purchasing domestic equity security

An investor purchasing a domestic equity security may be subject to a number of risks, but 2 of the most important of these risks include business risk and market risk. Any unexpected downward shifts in the financial performance, or projected financial performance, of the company will result in a reduction in the value of the equity security. Thus, the expected financial performance of the company will determine the expected return an investor requires on his investment. Additionally, the investor will be subject to risks that are systemic and not specific to the company issuing the equity security. These risks could include a terrorist attack or natural disaster. It's difficult to price this risk into a security at purchase and instead typically results in a sharply downward shift in security prices at the time of occurrence.

Expected return and risk

The relationship between risk and expected return is central to the evaluation of equity and fixed income investments. For equity securities, all else being equal, a security with greater risk (whether business risk, market risk, currency exchange risk, or others) will receive a lower price than an equity security with less risk. For fixed income investments, this variance in risk manifests itself through a difference in required yield. For instance, a fixed income security with greater risk must offer higher yields than a security with lower risks. In the secondary fixed income market, two securities with identical coupons may have different prices if one is considered to have a greater degree of risk than the other.

Auction markets

The primary feature of an auction market is that prices are set through a process whereby sellers enter offers, the amount and price at which they are willing to sell, and buyers enter bids, the amount and price at which they are willing to buy. Trades are executed when these bids and offers are matched up against each other. The Specialist or Market Maker is responsible for making a market in a given security. The Specialist/Market Maker's primary role is to match bids and offers to obtain the optimal pricing for both buyers and sellers. The goals of this process are to obtain better price discovery, improve liquidity, and dampen volatility. Bids and offers are prioritized first by price. The highest bids and lowest offers submitted will be executed first. The second step of prioritization is the time submitted. If multiple bids or offers are submitted at the same price, those that were submitted first will be executed first.

The largest and most well-known auction market within the United States is the New York Stock Exchange (NYSE). As of November in 2015, the companies listed on the NYSE totaled over $18.5 trillion in market capitalization and nearly 850 million trades had been placed during the year. While the NYSE has gradually moved toward a more automated and electronic trading system, the exchange still utilizes traders on the trading floor using the open outcry system where prices are negotiated and set by specialists and market makers.

Over-the-counter/negotiated market

One primary difference between an auction market and an over-the-counter or negotiated market is that an auction market typically has a physical location where buyers and sellers must converge to set prices. A negotiated market, however, need not have a centralized physical location as most of the buying and selling is done through dealers.

As mentioned above, prices in a negotiated market are largely set by dealers, who are primarily responsible for buying and selling securities in these markets. This is in stark contrast to an auction market, in which the buying and selling is performed by the traders or agents working on their behalf. Dealers in negotiated markets differ from brokers, market makers, or specialists in auction markets because instead of working to buy and sell on behalf of their clients (the investors) the dealers are buying and selling at their own risk for their own accounts.

The largest and most well-known over-the-counter or negotiated market in the United States is the NASD Automated Quotations system (NASDAQ). As of November in 2015, the companies listed on NASDAQ had a combined market capitalization of approximately $9 trillion. During 2015 alone, more than 1.2 billion shares were traded on the NASDAQ. While the number of trades placed nearly equals that of the larger NYSE, the total market capitalization of companies listed on the NYSE continues to exceed that of those listed on the NASDAQ by almost double, although there are a number of large companies on the NASDAQ, particularly technology companies. The key feature of the NASDAQ that differentiates it from the NYSE is the function of the dealers, who impact pricing by buying and selling securities from their own accounts, as opposed to market makers and brokers who work to match buyers and sellers at mutually agreeable prices within an auction market.

Differences between auction markets and negotiated markets

One key difference between an auction market and a negotiated, or over-the-counter, market is the role of dealers and market makers. In a negotiated market, dealers impact pricing by buying and selling securities from their own accounts, as opposed to market makers and brokers who work to match buyers and sellers at mutually agreeable prices within an auction market. Additionally, auction markets typically have a single physical location where traders come to match orders from buyers and sellers, where in a negotiated market this centralized physical location is not necessary and the buying and selling can be done over an electronic dealer network. As technology advances, the importance of a centralized physical location may be minimized, but at the present time, it does still play a role in the NYSE and traders physically interact on the trading floor.

New issue market

Most investors are familiar with secondary market transactions, in which a corporation's securities are purchased from another investor or a dealer. The primary market, or new issue market, is of critical importance to corporations as they raise money to finance their operations. When a corporation issues new securities (debt or equity), it can choose to issue through either a public offering or a private placement. In a private placement, all purchasers of the securities are qualified investors, such as banks, insurance companies, or large, sophisticated financial institutions. As such, the company can avoid many of the regulatory filings typically required. Alternatively, the company may choose to issue the securities through a public offering. To provide expertise in this distribution of securities and to ensure they receive the most competitive price available, companies will typically hire an investment bank to serve as an underwriter for the transaction. The investment bank will set the initial price for the securities and generate interest in the transactions to appropriately size the new issue.

Insider Trading and Securities Fraud Enforcement Act of 1988

The purpose of the Insider Trading and Securities Fraud Enforcement Act of 1988 was to broaden and strengthen regulatory and enforcement power previously provided under the Securities Exchange Act of 1934. The Act provided additional guidance and enforcement in a number of areas, including all of the following:
1. Broadening the scope of the legislation to include other firms or controlling persons who fail to take appropriate measures to prevent insider-trading violations
2. Increasing potential civil penalties for violations
3. Increasing potential criminal penalties and jail time for violations
4. Clarification around those traders who were impacted by violations and classified as contemporaneous traders
5. Providing that the SEC can award bounty payments of up to 10 percent of the civil penalty for providing information
6. Enacting a five-year statute of limitations after the date of the last transaction

Material, nonpublic information
The Insider Trading and Securities Fraud Enforcement Act of 1988 provides that every investment adviser "shall establish, maintain and enforce written policies and procedures reasonably designed, taking into consideration the nature of such investment adviser's business, to prevent the misuse in violation of this Act or the Securities Exchange Act of 1934, or the rules or regulations thereunder, of material, nonpublic information by such investment adviser or any person associated with such investment adviser." Material information is that which is likely to impact an investor's decision to invest in a security or the price that the investor is willing to pay to invest in a given security. Nonpublic information is information that has not been communicated to the general public or made available in public financial statements or press releases.

Civil and criminal penalties

The Insider Trading and Securities Fraud Enforcement Act of 1988 provides for a number of civil and criminal penalties for violations of the act and improper insider trading, including:

1. The SEC can impose damages against violators of the Act in an amount up to three times the profit gained or loss avoided as a result of the illegal transaction. These damages are limited to $1,000,000 for controlling persons.
2. Individuals may face fines of up to $1,000,000: the 1988 Act increased this limit from the previous limit of $100,000.
3. Non-natural persons may face fines of up to $2,500,000: the 1988 Act increased this limit from the previous limit of $500,000.
4. Violators may face a jail sentence of up to 10 years: the 1988 Act increased this limit from the previous limit of five years.

Contemporaneous traders

The Insider Trading and Securities Fraud Enforcement Act of 1988 provides for clearer interpretation and guidance around the rights of other investors who are impacted by violators of the Act. These other traders can fit into one of two categories: contemporaneous or non-contemporaneous. Contemporaneous traders are those who purchased the security in question (where the violation included a sale of security) or sold the security in question (where the violation included the purchase of a security). This clearer definition seeks to provide limits and minimize the number of people who can claim to have been impacted by changes in the price of the security. Non-contemporaneous traders are all other traders who may have been impacted, such as in the case of the purchase of a company where the price paid may have been impacted by the violation.

Controlling persons

A controlling person is defined as "every person who, directly or indirectly, controls any person liable under any provision of this title or of any rule or regulation thereunder." While this broad definition will be determined on a case-by-case basis, it will often include not only employers but also any other person with power to influence the activities of another person. The Insider Trading and Securities Fraud Enforcement Act of 1988 broadened the civil penalties that can be imposed upon controlling persons, including damages of up to three times the profit gained or loss avoided, up to a maximum of $1,000,000. In order to be found liable, a controlling person must have known or recklessly disregarded that fact that the controlled person was likely to engage in the acts constituting the violation and failed to prevent such acts. Additionally, a failure by the controlling person to establish policies and procedures to avoid such violations by controlled persons may also lead to liability.

Common stock

A share of common stock represents fractional ownership in the issuing company. As such, one feature of common stock is a voting right to elect the Board of Directors and other matters such as executive compensation and corporate financial policy. Another feature of common stock is the right to dividends and earnings of the company. Earnings that are reinvested into the company increase the value of the share price and dividends distributed are paid to common stockholders. Thus, common stockholders participate in the income earned by the company in one of those two methods. As a fractional owner in the company, common stockholders would receive a portion of the company's assets in the event of liquidation. However, common stockholders are at the lowest level of priority and will split only what is left after bondholders and preferred stockholders have collected their more senior debts.

Differences from preferred stock

Common stock differs from preferred stock in rights to dividends because preferred shares typically have a fixed, stated dividend while dividends for common shares can vary at the discretion of the company. Also, preferred shares have the first right to dividends and can also often have cumulative rights, so that any funds allocated to dividends will first be used to pay dividends, and any missed prior dividends, to preferred shareholders. Contrary to common stockholders, preferred stockholders typically do not have any voting rights. Finally, preferred shareholders would receive their portion of the liquidation prior to common stockholders in the event of corporate bankruptcy, giving them a greater level of principal protection. However, preferred stockholders still fall behind bondholders in the liquidation structure and would still face a substantial risk of loss.

Choosing preferred stock over common stock

One reason an investor may choose to invest in preferred stock as compared to a common stock is their desire for current income as opposed to capital appreciation. A share of preferred stock will generally pay a higher dividend rate than a share of common stock, but will not have the same possibility for upside capital appreciation through increased share price. Another incentive for investors to invest in preferred stock over common stock is the higher level of principal protection offered with preferred stock due to the order of dividend payments and the order of liquidation in the event of bankruptcy. Preferred stockholders receive their dividend payments before any payments are allocated to common stockholders and would also receive their share of a liquidation prior to any payments to common stockholders. Thus, an investor seeking a more conservative investment objective of current income or capital preservation might choose shares of preferred stock over common stock.

Convertible preferred stock

When preferred stock is said to be convertible, it means that the holder of the preferred stock can choose to convert his share of preferred stock into a given number of shares of common stock. For instance, suppose an investor purchases 10 shares of convertible preferred stock of Company A. Each share of preferred stock can be converted to 10 shares of common stock at the request of the investor. Now assume that Company A's common stock increases 300% in value over the next 12 months after the launch of a successful new product. Instead of continuing to receive the fixed dividend payment on his preferred shares, the investor can now participate in the upside of the common stock by converting each of his preferred shares into 10 shares of the common stock. However, if the common stock does not perform well, the investor could just maintain the preferred shares at the stated coupon rate. As one would imagine, this upside potential with downside protection is more expensive than a standard share of preferred stock and the price of the preferred shares will be largely driven by the expected performance of the underlying common stock.

ADRs

An American Depositary Receipt, or ADR, is a certificate issued by a US financial institution that represents a given number of shares of the equity securities of a foreign company. ADRs are denominated in US dollars and traded on US exchanges. ADRs simplify the process of investing in foreign companies for US investors by essentially removing the currency translation and international investing requirements. Thus, a US investor can still experience and participate in the performance of a foreign company without having to worry about foreign exchanges or personally handling the translation of foreign currency back into US dollars. For foreign companies, ADRs represent a simplified process for reaching a larger pool of investors without having to go through the same stringent requirements that would be imposed if they were to formally list their securities on a US exchange.

Rights, warrants, and options

A right is a security that gives the holder the ability to purchase a given number of shares at a predetermined price. The number of additional shares that can be purchased is typically in proportion to the number of shares already owned (i.e., an additional 10% purchase at $32.00) and the price included is typically at a discount to the current market price. A warrant is similar to a right in that it is offered and guaranteed directly by the issuing company and allows for the purchase of a specified number of shares at a given price. However, the time period within which a warrant is valid is typically much longer than that of a right or option. An option is a contract between two parties (not the issuing company) that gives the holder of the option the right, but not the obligation, to purchase a given number of securities from the other party at a specified date at an agreed upon price.

Secured and unsecured bonds

A secured bond is typically issued by a company that uses a particular asset or revenue stream as collateral for the bond as a means to lowering its interest payments. Because the principal value of the bond is "secured" by a specifically identified asset or the revenue stream, these bonds are less risky to investors than unsecured bonds so investors do not demand as high of an interest rate. An unsecured bond, however, does not have any specific assets or revenues backing it and the only security an investor has is that in the event of a bankruptcy or liquidation he will be in line ahead of equity security holders as a creditor of the company. All of the company's assets and revenue streams back all of its unsecured bonds. As such, investors will require higher yields on unsecured bonds and will typically be more concerned with the overall health of the company as opposed to the performance of a single asset or revenue stream.

Zero coupon bonds and convertible bonds

A zero coupon bond is a bond in which the investor pays a price that is discounted from the face amount of the bond and only receives repayment of the principal at the bond's maturity; this bond does not make any coupon payments. Thus, the duration of the bond is the remaining maturity since all payments occur at that time. This type of bond would be attractive to an investor who fears an upcoming fall in interest rates as it minimizes reinvestment risk. A convertible bond is a type of bond that the investor can choose to convert into a given number of common or preferred shares of the company's stock. This may be an attractive option for an investor who does not wish to take on the full risk of investing in the company's equity securities but wishes to retain the upside potential of the equity securities.

Mortgage-backed security and collateralized mortgage obligation

A mortgage-backed security (MBS) is a security with cash flows backed by a pool of mortgages with a given credit rating and expected prepayment rate. Payments of principal and interest on the mortgages are essentially passed through to the security holders. This type of security is attractive because it is often seen as a higher yielding instrument with relatively low principal risk because it is a secured obligation. A collateralized mortgage obligation (CMO) is a specific type of mortgage-backed security in which the bondholders are divided into tranches that determine the order in which they receive principal and interest payments. Because it is seen as a negative event to receive principal repayments earlier than expected, the most senior tranches are the last to receive principal repayments and are the first to receive interest payments. Investors in the more senior tranches typically receive higher rates than junior tranches because of the privileged repayment structure.

Treasury bills, treasury notes, and treasury bonds

Treasury bills are fixed income securities issued by the US government with durations of one year or less. Due to their short duration, these securities do not make coupon payments but are issued at a discount from par so that the return occurs through the increase from the purchase price to par over the duration of the security. Treasury notes are fixed income securities issued by the US government with durations of one to ten years and make semiannual coupon payments. Treasury bonds are fixed income securities issued by the US government with durations of greater than 10 years and make semiannual coupon payments. The primary difference between treasury bills, notes and bonds, and agency securities is that, unlike treasury securities that are issued by the US government and backed by the full faith of the US government, agency securities are backed by government-sponsored entities. The US government does not back or guarantee these securities and the risk of default is slightly higher than with treasury securities.

Treasury Inflation Protected Securities (TIPS)

Treasury Inflation Protection Securities (TIPS) were created to attract investors by offering protection against rising inflation, which erodes the value of fixed-income securities. Every six months, the interest rate paid on TIPS is adjusted to reflect changes in the Consumer Price Index (CPI). When inflation is rising, the interest payment paid on TIPS rises; if the CPI were to drop, interest payments would be lowered. Because of this built-in protection, TIPS are sold at lower interest rates than other government securities. Any rise in interest paid due to the adjustment is taxable in the year the adjustment is received.

Treasury receipts

Brokerage firms and other financial institutions may purchase Treasury notes and Treasury bonds and put them in trust. They then sell the receipts, or rights to individual interest or principal payments, to other investors. These are called Treasury receipts. However, unlike the original treasury bonds and notes, Treasury receipts are not backed by the full faith and credit of the U.S. government.

Separate Trading of Registered Interest and Principal Securities (STRIPS)

Separate Trading of Registered Interest and Principal Securities (STRIPS) are much like Treasury receipts, except that since the government has authorized stripping the securities into separate components, STRIPS are backed by the full faith and credit of the U.S. government.

Taxation of municipal bonds

One of the most attractive features of municipal bonds is that they are exempt from federal taxes and often also from state and local taxes. For investors in higher tax brackets, municipal bonds can be especially attractive when compared to fully taxable corporate bonds on a tax-equivalent yield basis. Additionally, while treasury securities are exempt at the federal level, they are still taxable at the state and local levels. However, agency securities, while taxable at the federal level, are exempt from taxes at the state and local levels. To summarize, corporate bonds and agency bonds are taxable at the federal level, while corporate bonds and treasury securities are taxable at the state and local levels. Keep in mind that there is some variation in the taxability of municipal bonds at the state and local levels and this is only a generalization.

General obligation bonds, revenue bonds, and industrial revenue bonds

General obligation bonds are issued without being associated with a specific project or revenue stream of the municipality. It is understood that these obligations will be met through the municipality's ability to generate revenue through taxation. Revenue bonds are issued to finance a particular revenue-generating project and the revenues from that project are specifically earmarked to repay the bondholders. These are generally longer term securities as the bonds cannot be repaid from the revenue source until the project has been completed and it is generating sufficient revenue to repay debt holders. Industrial revenue bonds are similar to revenue bonds in that the security is used to finance a revenue-generating project, the revenues of which are used to eventually repay debt holders. The primary difference is that industrial revenue bonds are typically issued by a municipality in conjunction with a private company that will also benefit from the undertaken project. The municipality is willing to partner with the private company in this project under the notion that the project will bring employment and revenue to the municipality and its constituents.

Money market funds

Money market funds play an important role for investors in providing both security of principal and liquidity. Specific examples of short-term instruments include:
- Treasury bills: fixed income securities issued by the US government with durations of one year or less. Due to their short duration, these securities do not make coupon payments but are issued at a discount from par so that the return occurs through the increase from the purchase price to par over the duration of the security.
- Certificates of deposit: securities issued by banks with fixed interest payments and maturities up to five years. Certificates of deposit are also guaranteed by the FDIC in the same way that banks accounts are protected.
- Commercial paper: fixed income securities issued by companies to finance short-term obligations. Commercial paper is issued at a discount to par and does not make interest payments. Durations of 270 days or less do not require registration with the SEC.

- Bankers acceptances: fixed income securities issued by firms to finance short-term obligations and are guaranteed by a commercial bank. Durations typically range only up to one year. Bankers acceptances are issued at a discount to par and do not make interest payments.

A money market fund seeks to maintain a net asset value of $1 per share while providing yield reflecting short-term market interest rates. In order to achieve this objective, money market funds may invest in short-term government securities, certificates of deposit, corporate commercial paper, and any other highly liquid, low risk securities. Money market funds play an important role in portfolio composition because their returns are very minimally correlated to the returns of other asset classes and as such, provide not only downside protection with low risk, but also serve as an important diversification tool. In addition to standard taxable money market funds, there are also tax-exempt money market funds that invest in short-term municipal debt that is exempt from federal taxes and may also be exempt from state and local taxes.

Diversified and non-diversified mutual funds

The investment universe provides for a wide array of available mutual funds, ranging from those that specialize in a given industry, sector, or valuation (non-diversified funds) to those that are meant to provide the investor with some level of risk mitigation through diversification, such as balanced funds or target date funds. In order to qualify as a diversified fund under the various tax and securities laws, a fund must meet the following requirements:
- Under the tax laws, for at least 75 percent of the portfolio:
  - Securities from one issuer may not represent more than 5 percent of the portfolio; and
  - No investment in the portfolio may represent more than 10 percent of the voting shares of the issuer.
- Under the securities laws, for at least 50 percent of the fund's net assets:
  - Securities from one issuer may not represent more than 5 percent of the portfolio; and
  - No investment in the portfolio may represent more than 10 percent of the voting shares of the issuer.
  - Securities from one issuer may not represent more than 25 percent of the fund's total assets.

Offering price of a mutual fund

The offering price, or public offering price, of a mutual fund is the price at which the fund can be purchased by an investor. The offering price may be identical to the net asset value (the total value of fund assets less expenses divided by the number of outstanding shares) or may differ depending upon whether any sales loads are charged. The offering price is simply equal to the net asset value plus any applicable

- 56 -

sales loads that the fund charges. For instance, Fund A's net asset value is $1,000 and Fund A charges a sales load of 5%. The offering price is calculated by taking the net asset value and dividing it by one minus the sales load: $1,000 dividend by (1 – 0.05) = $1,052.63. Investors can find the offering price of a security by calculating as shown above using the publicly reported and available net asset value and sales loads.

Share classes available within mutual funds

For most investors, there are three primary share classes available within mutual funds that provide for varying expense structures depending upon the investors expected holding period:

- Class A shares charge investors a front-end sales charge but typically charge lower annual 12b-1 fees than other share classes.
- Class B shares do not charge a front-end sales charge and instead impose a contingent deferred sales charge (CDSC) according to a defined schedule over the first several years of holding the fund (often six years). However, the annual 12b-1 fees imposed are higher than Class A shares. Once the CDSC no longer applies, the shares are converted into Class A shares, thereby lowering 12b-1 fees.
- Class C shares do not charge a front-end sales charge and usually impose some type of percentage-based fee if the shares are sold within a short time from the date of purchase (i.e., one year). Also, the 12b-1 fees are higher and the shares never convert into B shares or C shares.

Sales charges and expenses for mutual funds

Mutual funds contain a number of different fees and expenses, and it is important for investors to understand how each will impact their investment performance prior to selecting a fund.

- Front-End Sales Charge: This fee is imposed when Class A shares are purchased. If a fund's front-end sales charge is 5% and an investor purchases $1,000, then the investor will have $950 invested in the fund and will have paid a front-end sales charge of $50.
- Contingent Deferred Sales Charge (CDSC): A CDSC is normally imposed on Class B shares and follows a declining schedule as a percentage of assets redeemed. For instance, a CDSC of one percent in the third year and an investor redeems $1,000 worth of the fund's shares, then that investor will only receive $990 and will have paid $10 in CDSC.
- Asset Based Charges: Mutual funds also charge an amount against invested assets each year that includes charges related to management fees, marketing, and distribution fees (12b-1 fees), fees to the fund's investment adviser, transfer agent, and custodian, and any other operating expenses. In total, these fees are referred to as the expense ratio of the fund.

Role of dividends

Open-end investment companies, or mutual funds, distribute any dividends and realized capital gains back to investors as current income. Once this occurs, those distributions are no longer part of the fund's assets. However, this distribution has no impact on the total number of shares outstanding. As a result, any distributions of dividends and capital gains from the fund have the effect of reducing the net asset value, which is defined as the total assets held by the fund less operating expenses and divided by the number of outstanding shares. For mutual fund investors, a simple analysis of the change in the NAV may significantly understate the performance of the fund as these dividend and capital distributions must also be taken into account.

Benefits of breakpoints, rights of accumulation, and letters of intent

Breakpoints are frequently offered to investors purchasing Class A shares to minimize the impact of the front-end sales charge. Depending upon the specific fund family, a fund may offer specific increasing reductions in the front-end sales charge for larger purchases or with commitments to future purchases. Additionally, under rights of accumulation, many fund families will aggregate your current and previous transactions to reach a breakpoint level. For newer investors or those who plan to invest significantly more funds over time and want to receive the breakpoints now, a letter of intent is one way to achieve this outcome. A letter of intent commits the investor to making subsequent purchases in an amount equal to reach the breakpoint and provides for the discounted front-end sales charge as a result.

Letters of intent
Letters of intent allow investors to commit to a certain level of purchases over some specified future period of time (typically 90 days before the letter through 13 months following the letter) to achieve breakpoint pricing on front-end sales loads. If an investor unexpectedly is not able to complete all of the purchases required in the letter of intent to achieve the breakpoint pricing, the fund has the ability to retroactively apply the higher front-end sales charge that would have been collected. It is obviously in the best interest of both the investor and the fund company for letters of intent to be entered into only when there is a sincere intent to achieve the full purchase amount.

Rights of accumulation
Rights of Accumulation within the context of a mutual fund purchase refers to the practice whereby a mutual fund family will consider other purchases and other current holdings in determining whether or not an investor qualifies for breakpoint pricing on the front-end sales charge. The fund family will look at the total amount you have invested in the past, and may also be willing to consider amounts invested in other asset classes and styles under the same fund family, other types of accounts you hold whether retirement or education savings accounts, and accounts of direct family members such as spouses or children. However, each fund family differs in

their treatment of account combination and qualifying groups so investors should review this information carefully. For instance, valuation methods used for historical purchases may include historical cost, the current net asset value, or the current public offering price.

Differences between letters of intent and rights of accumulation

Letters of intent and rights of accumulation are both tools that can be utilized by investors to achieve discounted "breakpoint" pricing on front-end sales charges for new purchases. However, they differ significantly in terms of who would benefit from each. Letters of intent are much more beneficial for newer investors to a fund family who plan to make regular and/or significant contributions over the near-term (13 months). Rights of accumulation, on the other hand, benefit investors who have a long history with a given fund family and have accumulated a large amount of assets under management with the firm. Both groups are important to the fund family and these discounts are offered to entice new investors to channel a greater proportion of their invested assets to a given investment company and then to keep that investor happy by continuing to lower future front-end sales charges on subsequent purchases.

Redemption of mutual fund shares

Contrary to an investment in an equity or fixed income security of a single issuer, investors in mutual funds have the ability to redeem either whole or fractional shares. This is particularly beneficial for smaller investors in their establishment of diversified investment portfolios. If investors had to purchase whole shares of each underlying security within a portfolio, it would be extremely difficult to manage asset allocation and would result in significant fund requirements to make additional purchases or liquidate positions. However, with fractional shares in mutual funds, investors can manage their holdings down to the penny. This allows investors with smaller investable asset bases to better manage their asset allocations and properly allocate future purchases and dividend reinvestments.

Signature guarantee

In order to process certain mutual fund transactions, such as redemptions of shares within a short time frame following a change of address or bank account information, a fund company can require the investor to provide a signature guarantee. A signature guarantee is a written endorsement from an eligible institution certifying that the signature on the redemption request is valid. Particularly in the case of a mutual fund redemption shortly after account information has been changed or updated, this provides both the fund company and the investor with important fraud protection and peace of mind in knowing that any transactions submitted have to be approved and certified as being legitimate.

Example redemption request

Suppose Mr. Smith submits a redemption request for his entire mutual fund balance at 2:00 p.m. on January 1. He currently holds 100 shares of Fund A. At 4:00, the market closes and Fund A's NAV is calculated based on closing prices for each of the underlying securities and any applicable fund operating expenses. Let's assume the NAV as of the close of business on January 1 is $10.00. The amount of the liquidation is 100 shares multiplied by $10 per share, for a total of $1,000.00. However, Fund A has a Contingent Deferred Sales Charge of 1.00%. In order to collect this charge, Fund A will reduce the amount that is distributed to Mr. Smith so that the payment from Fund A to Mr. Smith upon redemption is only $990 ($1,000 multiplied by 99%). Mutual funds must make payment of the redemption to investors within seven calendar days from the date on which the redemption request was submitted.

Professional investment management

Mutual funds are an important tool to individual investors because it allows them access to industry experts at a relatively low cost. For instance, to properly construct a portfolio without mutual funds, an investor would need to conduct extensive due diligence on a number of individual debt and equity securities. This process would require an inordinate amount of time and skill in relation to the size of the average investor's typical investment. With mutual funds, however, that individual can now determine that he wants exposure to large cap value stocks for one half of his portfolio and high-yield bonds for the other half. Instead of researching individual securities, he can invest in a mutual fund where a team of portfolio managers and research analysts who are experts in that sector of the market have conducted the due diligence and perform ongoing monitoring to ensure exposure to only the best securities within that sector. Since the costs of the fund's research and transactions are shared across many investors, the cost to individual investors is much lower.

Clearly stated investment objectives

It is critically important for each fund to have a clearly stated investment objective outlined in the prospectus and statement of additional information so that investors have a clear expectation of the objectives and constraints of the fund. A fund's investment objectives should also specify the types of securities in which the fund will invest. While the portfolio manager and research analysts retain discretion over the securities in which they invest, they must remain within the stated objectives of the fund. For instance, if an investor's chooses to invest in ABC Small Cap Growth Fund, the fund must continue to invest in the best available small cap growth funds. If the fund began investing in mid cap or value securities, this fund would have what is known as "style drift." With style drift, investors in a fund may find themselves over- or under-weight in certain asset classes and investment styles.

Timing of investment decisions

The timing of investment decisions is critically important to a mutual fund investor in two different ways: the readiness of liquidity of the mutual fund and the ability for the mutual fund to act quickly on changes to economic or company financial information. Mutual funds provide significant liquidity to investors because of the fact that their funds are pooled with a significant number of other investors and each individual investor's share of the total assets represents a very small proportion of total assets in the fund. Thus, one investor can quickly and easily liquidate his position in the fund without impacting the price of the fund or underlying securities and the investor knows he will know almost the exact price he will receive. Additionally, whereas an individual investor may take several days or even weeks to process changing company and economic financial information and implementing those changes to the portfolio, an individual investor who invests in a mutual fund will experience the benefit of a team of analysts constantly monitoring and evaluating the investment portfolio and economic climate.

Financial and economic research

An individual investor who is trying to construct his investment portfolio must dedicate significant time and resources into financial and economics research. The resources include both the time to dedicate to the research, which can be significant, and monetary resources to subscribe to various financial websites and research tools. Thus, an investor who is able to invest in a diversified mutual fund can essentially outsource the time and information requirements to the qualified team of portfolio managers and analysts. Instead of analyzing each individual security, the individual investor must now only research and evaluate the portfolio manager and the risk-adjusted returns and style consistency of the fund. Because of the number of investors who share these same fixed costs of the fund, the individual investor can achieve significant efficiencies as a result.

Equity income fund

Equity income mutual funds seek to provide return to investors through a combination of equity dividends and capital appreciation. Proportionately, more of the fund's returns will come from equity dividends and the fund will not rely as significantly upon capital appreciation as most other equity funds. Additionally, these funds are typically less aggressive than a fund that provides return solely through capital appreciation. In order to provide a consistent and growing level of income through dividends, equity income funds typically invest in relatively stable companies with a long history of consistent and growing dividend yields. In selecting the individual securities for the fund, the research team must consider both the prospects for the dividend return, but also ensure that the fund will not be taking unnecessary risks as it relates to capital appreciation. Investors in equity income funds will typically be classified as moderate due to their desire for the security of current income through dividends while retaining some potential for capital appreciation.

Equity growth fund

Equity growth funds seek to provide returns through capital appreciation. While the fund may hold some securities that pay modest dividends, the dividends are not a significant source of returns for the fund. Instead, the portfolio manager and research team attempt to identify securities that will grow (and whose stock price will appreciate) at a rate greater than that which is implied through the current stock price. Investors in equity growth funds are typically more aggressive and may be investing over a longer time horizon or with a greater target return than investors in fixed income or equity income funds. These investors are also subject to greater risk through capital losses as the companies in which these funds invest are oftentimes less established and more volatile.

Equity income/growth fund

Equity income/growth funds seek to provide returns through a balanced combination of equity dividends and capital appreciation. Stable large-cap equity securities are the most common type of investment in equity growth/income funds because they are able to provide a significant source of current income through consistent divided yields while also retaining exposure to capital appreciation potential through increases in the price of the common stock. The equity/growth income fund differs from strictly an equity growth fund through its greater focus on providing for current income. Similarly, the equity growth/income fund differs from strictly an equity income fund because equity income funds would often include bonds and equity securities with less expected return through capital appreciation. This type of fund may appeal to an older investor who seeks some stability through current dividend income, but also needs to achieve a higher level of return than can be provided by bond yields alone.

Equity aggressive growth fund

Equity aggressive growth funds seek to provide the highest level of return achievable through rapid capital appreciation. Portfolio managers and research analysts for aggressive growth funds seek to identify companies whose growth prospects are significant and whose stock valuations are expected to rapidly appreciate. As a result, the companies identified as having these tremendous growth prospects are typically small and mid-cap companies who are less established and can increase their revenue and profits by multiples of their current levels, not single percentages as can be expected for more well-established large cap companies. Alongside the higher expected return comes higher risk and volatility. It is precisely because of the inherent risk and unknown future prospects for these companies that both the upside and downside risk are so significant. Also, portfolio management is

- 62 -

even more important in these funds as many of the target companies are the subjects of less research coverage.

Equity value fund

Equity value funds seek to provide returns through capital appreciation on funds that are considered to be currently undervalued. Oftentimes, these funds invest in companies that are undervalued due to current business or economic conditions that are expected to reverse course at some point in the near future and allow for higher valuations. For instance, a value fund will seek companies with a low price-to-earnings ratio as compared to its peers, if the fund believes that company's valuation does not deserve to be discounted, or does not believe the company's valuation deserves to be discounted to the extent that it has been. Thus, the capital appreciation returns earned by this fund will come both through the natural cycle of corporate earnings and economic growth, but also by a return of the company to a higher relative valuation.

Equity blend/core fund

Equity blend or core funds provide a mix of returns through investing in companies that could be considered either growth or value funds, or balanced between the two approaches. Instead of limiting the choice of underlying investments to specifically identifying growth or value companies, blend or core funds seek to provide the highest risk-adjusted return through investing in companies with the best potential risk-adjusted returns, regardless of whether they are undervalued or underestimated in terms of future growth. By not placing the restrictions on the source of the growth, investors in blend or core funds can get the best funds from both approaches in a single fund. Thus, the fund may include a company whose price-to-earnings ratio is half that of its peers but is about to launch a new product that will improve its competitive position, thereby raising the ratio to the industry standard and providing significant earnings to stockholders. That same fund may also include a start-up technology company that may currently be overvalued relative to current earnings, but which is expected to become the next Facebook.

Equity balanced fund

A balanced fund seeks to provide returns to investors through a number of different sources. The idea behind this is that the investor should achieve a fully diversified fund and risk should be minimized as a result, because of the "balance" across asset classes, valuations, and styles. Typically, balanced funds will invest in a mixture of growth equities, value equities, corporate bonds, government bonds, and short-term instruments with a goal of providing diversification across these multiple asset classes. While the result may be lower returns as compared with some focused, all-equity funds, these funds are essentially seeking to provide a moderate level of return (somewhere between all fixed income and all equity) while minimizing risk.

Comparing equity mutual funds based on investment style

Although there are numerous sub-classifications of equity mutual fund investment styles, funds are typically grouped into one of three categories based on a valuation approach and one of three categories based on capitalization. The three valuation approaches are value, growth, and blend. Value funds are those that primarily invest in securities that the portfolio management team believes to be undervalued considering business conditions and valuations of competitors. It is believed that these securities will outperform their peers over time as their valuations rise back into line with broader industry and market trends. Growth funds, on the other hand, are those that invest in companies believed to have growth prospects that are not fully reflected in the current pricing of the securities. Oftentimes, these are technology companies or those in other industries whose valuation may significantly increase based upon the successful launch of a new technology or new product. A blend fund seeks to invest in the best of both growth and value companies without a distinct preference between the two. Further, each fund is classified by the size of the companies in whose securities it typically invests. Opinions vary, but small caps are typically considered to be less than $2 billion in total market capitalization, mid caps between $2 billion and $10 billion, and large caps over $10 billion.

Total return and after-tax return of a fund

While the total return of the fund is important, an investor will ultimately only receive the after-tax return. Thus, an investor should prefer a fund with a higher after-tax return, regardless of the comparison between pre-tax returns. A fund's total return is calculated as the growth in the NAV plus any distributions (i.e., dividends, capital gains, and interest distributed) divided by the beginning NAV. To calculate the after-tax return, multiply the pre-tax total return by one minus the investor's marginal income tax rate. Funds with identical total returns could differ substantially in terms of after-tax returns for different investors. For example, an investor in a 20% marginal personal income tax bracket will achieve a higher after-tax return than an investor in a 35% marginal personal income tax bracket. As another example, let's say an investor is choosing between Fund A and Fund B. He expects both funds to yield a return of 5% per year, but Fund A's yield is primarily derived from dividends while Fund B's yield is primarily derived from capital appreciation. The investor will receive a greater after-tax return on Fund B as a result of the lower tax rate on long-term capital gains than on dividends, which are taxed as ordinary income.

NAV

The net asset value (NAV) of a mutual fund is equivalent to an equity security's stock price; that is, it represents the current cost/value to an investor of one share. The net asset value of a mutual fund is calculated by summing up the value of all of the securities held, subtracting out any liabilities and the operating expenses of the

- 64 -

fund, and then dividing the result by the number of outstanding shares. Unlike stock prices, which adjust throughout the day, the net asset value is only calculated daily. A more frequent calculation would be extremely cumbersome, both for the investment company and for investors. The NAV is calculated once the market closes each day with the closing security prices as of that day. That is the NAV that is in effect for the following trading day.

Taxable fixed income fund

Taxable fixed income funds seek to provide current income to bondholders through periodic coupon payments on the underlying bonds that are purchased by the fund. In a taxable fund, these underlying bonds typically include corporate bonds, the income derived from which is taxable at the federal, state, and local levels. Depending upon the goal and target return of the individual fund, the mix between corporate, treasury, and agency securities and the durations of the underlying securities will vary. Funds that seek to provide higher returns will typically have longer durations and be comprised of lower quality, higher yielding corporate bonds. To the contrary, funds prioritizing preservation of capital over current income will invest in bonds with shorter durations and higher credit quality, such as treasury bills or agency securities.

Tax exempt fixed income fund

Tax exempt income funds seek to provide tax-exempt current income by investing in municipal bonds, which are exempt from federal income taxes and also frequently from state and local income taxes. For investors in higher tax brackets, municipal bonds can be especially attractive when compared to fully taxable corporate bonds on a tax-equivalent yield basis. For instance, consider an investor whose combined marginal personal income tax rate is 30%. When that investor earns a 7% yield on a corporate bond, the after-tax return to the investor is only 4.9%. Thus, the investor can earn just as high of an after-tax return through investing in a municipal bond yielding 4.9%. The higher the investor's marginal tax rate, the more of an advantage the tax-exemption provides to the investor.

High yield fixed income fund

A high yield fixed income fund seeks to provide a high level of current income to investors by investing in fixed income securities with higher current yields. The most common reason for these securities to have higher yields is that there is greater concern about the issuing company's ability to meet the ongoing coupon payment obligations. Just as with equity securities, an investor must take greater risk to achieve greater return. With fixed income securities, the increased risk is in the form of default risk, or the risk that the company will fail to make coupon payments or repay the par value of the security at maturity. Investors may feel that high yield bonds provide an enhanced return over typical corporate bonds while still taking a lower level of risk than in an equity portfolio.

Strategy differences between taxable, tax exempt, and high yield fixed income funds

Taxable fixed income funds typically invest in corporate, treasury, and agency securities, income from which is taxable at the federal level. These funds are appealing to investors as they provide a balanced mix of return through current income with capital preservation and safety. Tax-exempt fixed income funds typically invest in municipal bonds, which are exempt from federal income taxes, and often state and local taxes as well. Tax-exempt funds are extremely appealing to investors in higher tax brackets, who can achieve an even greater benefit on these funds as compared to taxable investments than can other investors.
High yield bonds seek to provide greater current income levels to investors by investing in the fixed income securities of companies who may be at a greater risk of default. High yield bonds are appealing to investors who are seeking to earn current income but seek a higher return than that offered through traditional corporate bonds. For those investors willing to accept an additional level of risk, the payoff of high yield bonds can be quite attractive.

Industry concentration fund and asset allocation fund

An industry (or sector) concentration fund will invest in the securities of companies from a given industry at a significantly greater proportion than what the companies represent in terms of a given index or the broader market. Thus, if an investor thought that the automotive industry was going to outperform relative to the rest of the market, he may choose to invest in an automotive concentration fund to increase his exposure to that industry. An asset allocation fund seeks to provide investors with a given asset allocation, often determined by level of risk (i.e., conservative or aggressive). These funds are attractive to investors who want a diversified portfolio with a given level of risk, but would prefer to turn over the selection of individual securities to a professional.

Geographic concentration fund and international fund

A geographic concentration fund will invest heavily in the securities of companies that are located in a given geographic area. As an example, suppose an investor believes that certain geopolitical events will cause companies in Eastern Europe to have significant growth opportunities. In order to increase his exposure to this growth, he would seek to invest in a fund that is concentrated in this region. An international fund, for an investor in the United States, would invest primarily in securities issued by companies outside of the United States. This is not to be confused with a global fund, which would invest across international and domestic companies in proportion to their share of the world markets.

Mortgage backed securities fund and index fund

A mortgage backed securities fund will invest in a pool of underlying mortgages, and the payments from the fund to investors represent a pass through of mortgage interest and principal repayments. The higher credit quality of the fund, the lower the rates that will be offered. Additionally, mortgage backed securities can be further divided into more specific funds, such as agency mortgage backed securities and commercial mortgage backed securities. An index fund will seek to replicate the performance of a given index by investing in a representative cross section of the funds contained in the index. The goal of the fund is to minimize costs while providing a close replication of performance, so it would be too costly to invest in each individual security contained in the index and adjust the proportions held. For the Russell 2000, an index fund would merely seek to replicate the portfolio's characteristics using a fraction of the underlying funds, as opposed to buying all 2000 securities.

Precious metals fund, funds of funds, and principal-protected funds

A precious metals fund would invest in companies that are involved in the mining and exploration of precious metals. The performance of such securities is dependent not only upon the operational success of the company, but also on commodity prices for the various precious metals that they mine. A fund of funds is a mutual fund that seeks to provide returns to investors by investing in an array of hedge funds. The advantage of this type of fund to the average investor is that by pooling their money together with other investors through the fund of funds, they are able to access hedge funds and share classes that they would not have had access to because of high initial investment requirements. Principal protected funds seek to invest in underlying debt and equity securities while offering a guarantee of your initial investment principal through an arrangement with an insurance company. These funds often have lengthy lock-up periods where you cannot access your funds without penalty and often have high fees. An investor ends up paying for the guarantee of principal protection.

Comparing funds on the basis of investment objective

Before an investor begins looking at various analytical and quantitative comparisons across funds, the investor must select funds that align with his or her objectives. Each open-end investment company, or mutual fund, will have a stated investment objective (usually only a sentence or two in length) that will provide investors with an overview of the fund's goals. Investment objectives typically provide an indication as to which of the following are most important to the fund: preservation of principal, current income, capital appreciation, or liquidity. The investment objective of a fund is critical to the operation of the fund and provides the context within which all other strategies and risks can be evaluated. Also, the investment objective of a mutual fund is rarely modified, and can be modified only with shareholder approval.

ETF and hedge fund

An exchange-traded fund (ETF) is a relatively newer type of security that seeks to replicate the performance of a given index or commodity. ETFs are valued throughout the day just as any other security would be and typically have very low fees as the investor is not paying for active management as he would be with most mutual fund investments. A hedge fund is quite the opposite. Hedge funds seek unconventional sources of outperformance by picking individual stocks or market movements to exploit. Unlike an ETF, which is valued throughout each day and allows an investor to buy as little as one share, hedge funds are valued much less frequently, often monthly, and typically require substantial minimum investments. Hedge funds also offer significantly less liquidity as investments may be subject to long restricted periods where the investor cannot access his funds. The primary factor in deciding between these two investment alternatives comes down to whether that investor believes that the market is efficient, or at least close, or whether that investor thinks that active management can provide a superior return.

Holding period of securities

The holding period of a mutual fund is defined as the time from the date of acquisition to the date of redemption of the fund. Additionally, the fund itself will have holding periods for each of its underlying securities, also calculated as the time from the date of acquisition to the date of redemption. When a security is owned for less than one year, it is classified as short-term capital gains. Distributions that are the result of short-term capital gains as well as interest and dividend income are all taxed in the same way as dividends at ordinary income tax rates. Distributions resulting from long-term capital gains, those arising from the sale of securities held for more than one year, receive preferential tax treatment and are taxed at lower long-term capital gains tax rates.

Wash sale rule

The Securities Exchange Commission defines a wash sale as occurring when an investor sells a position in a security at a loss and within 30 days following the sale either (i) buys substantially identical stocks or securities, (ii) acquires substantially identical stock or securities in a fully taxable trade, or (iii) acquires a contract or option to buy substantially identical stock or securities. Without the "wash sale rule," which prohibits the investor from claiming the loss as a deduction on his tax return, an investor would be able to essentially capitalize on his loss position without changing his investment position. By taking losses on the sale of the security and then reestablishing his position in the security, the investor would be converting unrealized losses to realized losses in the current tax year, then downward adjusting his tax basis and deferring the higher potential tax gains to later years.

FINRA's Rule 2000 Duties and Conflicts

FINRA's Rule 2000 outlines six components of standards of conduct and duties to customers and is important in defining and shaping the way in which financial professionals conduct themselves. Specifically, the six rules are:

- Rule 2010 Standards of Commercial Honor and Principles of Trade: states that members should act justly and equitably in their business dealings.
- Rule 2020 Use of Manipulative, Deceptive, or Other Fraudulent Devices: states that members should not use any manipulative or deceptive means to effect transactions.
- Rule 2060 Use of Information Obtained in Fiduciary Capacity: delineates the additional responsibilities imposed upon one acting in a fiduciary capacity, specifically with respect to the use of information to solicit sales.
- Rule 2070 Transactions Involving FINRA Employees: outlines the procedures to be followed when a member is involved in a security or transactions involving a FINRA employee.
- Rule 2080 Obtaining an Order of Expungement of Customer Dispute Information from the Central Registration Depository (CRD) System: outlines the policies and procedures for removing a customer dispute from a member's record.
- Rule 2090 Know Your Customer: is one of the more well-known FINRA rules and states that a member has a responsibility to use reasonable diligence to know all pertinent facts about customers to be able to make suitable recommendations.

Violation of rules

The first example of a way in which a member could violate one of the Rule 2000 mandates is through the use of fraudulent activities as prohibited in Rule 2020. A member would be in violation of Rule 2020 if he used falsified financial statements in order to entice a customer to invest in a particular security. Another example of a violation would be a circumstance in which a member failed to properly know his customer, recommending a highly volatile security for an investor who had a short-term time horizon and need for principal protection. Simple due diligence and interviews with the customer would have revealed this information. The final example is the case of an investor's fiduciary passing along confidential information that was obtained through his fiduciary duties to a salesman within his company who uses that information to develop a custom sales proposal, without the customer's consent. This would be a violation of Rule 2060 and an improper use of the information obtained through his fiduciary capacity.

FINRA Rule 2150

Pursuant to FINRA Rule 2150, no member or associated person is permitted to guarantee a customer against losses in a securities transaction. The goal of this prohibition is to ensure that the member or associated person does not become a party to the transaction in a greater role, that of guarantor. The security being purchased, and all of its risks are outlined in the security's prospectus and statement of additional information and the member or associated person must not provide any additional incentives or guarantees to entice the customer to purchase the security. As it relates to sharing in the profits and losses in a customer's account, FINRA Rule 2150 prohibits this unless:

1. The associated person receives prior written authorization from both the member and the customer and the associated person shares in the performance of the account in direct proportion to the contributions made to the account by that person; or
2. The associated person is sharing in the account with immediate family and receives prior written approval from both the member and the customer.

Variable contracts of an insurance company

FINRA Rule 2320 Variable Contracts of an Insurance Company applies only to variable contracts, which are defined as "contracts providing for benefits or values which may vary according to the investment experience of any separate or segregated account or accounts maintained by an insurance company." Whole life insurance contracts, in which the cash value is determined based on the age and gender of the insured in relation to the face amount of the contract, would not be governed under this rule. Along the same lines, a universal life insurance policy is credited with a rate declared by the insurance carrier. This rate is often determined based on the performance of the carrier's general account, the assets of which back the liability from the policy. Thus, there is no separate account created for these cash values and the policy is not subject to this rule. A term life insurance policy requires the policyholder to pay a fixed premium for a given number of years to maintain a given level of insurance coverage. These policies have no cash value, and thus are not covered under this rule. In a variable universal life insurance policy, the policyholder has the ability to invest the cash value of the policy in a number of separate accounts. This is the only type of insurance policy that is covered by Rule 2320.

As provided in FINRA Rule 2320 Variable Contracts of an Insurance Company:
- The term "purchase payment" shall mean the consideration paid at the time of each purchase or installment for or under the variable contract.
- The term "variable contracts" shall mean contracts providing for benefits or values that may vary according to the investment experience of any separate or segregated account or accounts maintained by an insurance company.
- The term "affiliated member" shall mean a member that, directly or indirectly, controls, is controlled by, or is under common control with a non-member company.
- The term "cash compensation" shall mean any discount, concession, fee, service fee, commission, asset-based sales charge, loan, override, or cash employee benefit received in connection with the sale and distribution of

variable contracts. "Non-Cash Compensation" is all other forms of compensation, including merchandise, gifts and prizes, travel expenses, meals, and lodging.

- The term "offeror" shall mean an insurance company, a separate account of an insurance company, an investment company that funds a separate account, any adviser to a separate account of an insurance company or an investment company that funds a separate account, a fund administrator, an underwriter, and any affiliated person of such entities.

FINRA Rule 2320 deems that payment has been received at the time at which the purchase payment has been submitted and the insurance application has been submitted to and accepted by the insurance carrier. However, in certain instances the payment may be considered to have been received when the payment is actually made, if both parties agree to the timing as such. Due to the fact that payment is not considered to have been received until the application has also been submitted and accepted, it is incumbent upon the member to submit as promptly as possible to the issuer the completed application and the purchase payment, or at least a significant enough portion of the purchase payment to issue the policy.

FINRA Rule 2320 states that no member who is a principal underwriter is permitted to sell variable contracts through a different broker dealer unless the following conditions are met:
1. The broker dealer through which the underwriter is selling must be a member; and
2. There must be an existing sales agreement in place between the underwriter and the broker dealer.

The rule also places restrictions upon members relating to their participation in the offering or sale of variable contracts. Members are not allowed to participate unless the insurance company, upon receipt of a properly completed request for redemption in accordance with the terms of the contract, makes prompt payment for the amounts requested in accordance with the contract terms, prospectus, and Investment Company Act.

FINRA Rule 2320 provides for certain restrictions and limitations on the circumstances and types of compensation that can be paid to members and associated persons for the sale of variable contracts, as follows:
1. No associated person of a member shall accept any compensation from anyone other than the member with which the person is associated.
2. No member or person associated with a member shall accept any compensation from an offeror in the form of securities.
3. Members are obligated to maintain records of all compensation received by the member or its associated persons and such records shall include the names of the offerors, names of the associated persons, and amounts of cash and non-cash compensation.

4. No member or associated person shall make or receive payments of non-cash compensation, unless it is under one of the following arrangements:
   a. Annual gifts per person do not exceed FINRA limits and are not based on achievement of sales targets
   b. An occasional meal, ticket, or comparable entertainment that is infrequent and not meant to raise any question of impropriety
   c. Reimbursement for training or education

Members' responsibilities regarding deferred variable annuities

Application - this rule applies to recommended purchases and exchanges of deferred variable annuities and recommended initial subaccount allocations. The Rule states that documents can be created, stored, and transmitted in electronic or paper form, and electronic signatures are acceptable as well as written form.
Principal review and approval - before submitting a customer's application to an insurance company for processing, a member must have the application package approved by a registered principal.
Supervisory procedures - a member must implement procedures for surveillance to determine if associated persons have rates of effecting deferred variable annuity exchanges that raise for review, whether such rates are consistent with FINRA or SEC rules. A member must also have policies and procedures designed to implement corrective measures addressing inappropriate exchanges.
Training - a member must develop and document training policies or programs designed to ensure that associated persons who effect and registered persons who review transactions of deferred variable annuities are compliant.

Non-qualified deferred compensation

Non-qualified deferred compensation plans allow a select group of management and highly compensated employees the opportunity to defer income on a pre-tax basis. In order to maintain its exemption from the Employee Retirement Income Security Act of 1974 (ERISA), these plans must remain unfunded. In the event of company insolvency, a participant in a non-qualified plan will be a general unsecured creditor of the company. Non-qualified deferred compensation plans differ from a 401(k) plan in a number of respects, including the ability to withdraw funds prior to age 59½ without an early withdrawal penalty, no IRS limitations on the amounts that can be contributed, and balances may not be rolled over into an IRA. Benefit payments made to participants are taxed as ordinary income when received. Following a number of corporate scandals, Internal Revenue Code Section 409A was enacted as part of the American Jobs Creation Acts in 2004, restricting a participant's ability to modify, and more specifically to accelerate, the time and form of payment previously elected.

Impact of ERISA and Internal Revenue Code Section 409A
In order to avoid having to comply with the eligibility requirements of ERISA, non-qualified deferred compensation plans must remain unfunded, so that in the event

of the insolvency of the plan sponsor, the employee would be a general creditor. As a result, non-qualified deferred compensation plans are typically offered to only a select group of management and other highly compensated employees, typically representing 10% or less of the total workforce. As a result of much of the scrutiny of executive pay following certain high-profile incidents (i.e., Enron, WorldCom, etc.), legislation was passed to enact Internal Revenue Code Section 409A, which imposed more stringent limitations around the timing and modification of distribution elections under a non-qualified plan. Section 409A specifies only a handful of distribution events under which a participant can receive payment, including separation from service, change in control, death, disability, and financial hardship. Additionally, the timing and form of payment must be specified prior to the deferral of the compensation. Code Section 409A also limits modifications so that any new payment timing submitted must be elected at least 12 months prior to the previously scheduled date of payment and must delay payment by at least five years from the originally scheduled date.

Tax treatment for deferrals, earnings on deferrals, and benefit distributions

Within a non-qualified deferred compensation plan, an employee's deferrals of compensation are not taxed as income. However, it is important to note that FICA taxes (social security and Medicare) are still taken from the employee's pay at the time of deferral. The notional account into which the employee has deferred compensation grows tax-deferred until the time of distribution. At the time of distribution, the payment is treated as ordinary income. However, since FICA was collected at the time of deferral, the distribution is not subject to FICA. For the plan sponsor of a non-qualified deferred compensation plan, there is a lost tax deduction because the income was never actually paid to the employee. However, the company must recognize an immediate liability on their balance sheet equal to the amount of the deferral. There is an additional balance sheet item to represent the future tax deferral that will be credited upon payment of the benefit to the participant, so this lost tax deduction is only a cash flow concern.

"Breakpoint" sales

"Breakpoint" sales (FINRA Rule 2342) - a member is not to sell investment company shares at a price below the point that the sales charge is reduced on quantity transactions in order to gain the applicable higher sales charges.

Prompt payment for investment company shares (NASD Rule 2830) - a member engaging in retail transactions for investment company shares are to transmit payments from customers for the shares to the payees by the later of either the end of the 3rd business day after the order to purchase, or the end of one business day after receipt of the payment from the customer.

Influencing or rewarding employees of others

Influencing or rewarding employees of others (FINRA Rule 3220) - a member is not to give anything of value in excess of $100 per individual per person per year in relation to the business of the employer.

Arbitration disclosure to associated persons signing or acknowledging Form U4 (FINRA Rule 2263) - a member is to provide an associated person with a specific written statement at any time the person is asked to sign or initial a Form U4. This statement ensures the person understands predispute arbitration.

Borrowing from or lending to customers

As stated in FINRA Rule 3240, borrowing from or lending to customers is prohibited unless:
1. The member maintains written procedures for such transactions
2. The borrowing or lending arrangement is with a customer who is immediate family or with a customer who is a financial institution in the business of providing credit or loans
3. The customer is a registered person with the same member firm
4. The lending arrangement is based on a personal relationship with the customer
5. The lending arrangement is based on a business relationship outside of the broker-customer relationship.

These guidelines are meant to protect the broker-customer relationship and to ensure that all transactions between the two parties fit within the scope of appropriate transactions that are covered within the regulatory guidelines.

Limitations imposed on dealing with non-member brokers or dealers

NASD Rule 2420 states that members shall deal with non-members at the same prices, fees, and terms and commissions as in their dealings with the general public. Additionally, the rule states that no member shall:
1. In any transaction with any non-member broker or dealer, allow or grant to such non-member broker or dealer any selling concession, discount, or other allowance allowed by such member to a member of a registered securities association and not allowed to a member of the general public
2. Join with any non-member broker or dealer in any syndicate or group contemplating the distribution to the public of any issue of securities or any part thereof
3. Sell any security to or buy any security from any non-member broker or dealer except at the same price at which at the time of such transaction such member would buy or sell such security, as the case may be, from or to a person who is a member of the general public not engaged in the investment banking or securities business

NASD Rules IM-2420-1 and IM-2420-2

Transactions between members and non-members (IM-2420-1)
A. Certain non-members of the Association are: persons excluded from the definition of member in Rule 0120, expelled dealers, suspended dealers, broker or dealer with registration revoked by the SEC, and a broker or dealer with membership cancelled or resigned.
B. Exempted securities/transactions - the Rule does not apply to exempted securities defined in Section 3(a)(12) of the Act. The Rule does not apply to transactions enacted on an exchange.
C. Over-the-counter transactions in securities other than exempted securities - a member is not to participate in a selling group with a non-member to acquire and distribute an issue of securities. If a member is participating as part of a selling group, the member is not to allow any selling concession or discount to a bank or trust company. A member may not participate in a selling group with a suspended or expelled dealer.
Continuing commission policy (IM-2420-2) - payment of continuing commission is allowed, as long as the commission is being received by a member. If such person ceases to become a member, the payments must stop.

Suitability

MSRB Rule G-19 requires that, prior to trading in a retail customer's account, the registered individual must collect suitability information regarding the customer's financial status, tax status, investment objective concerning the municipal security being traded, and any other information that might be required to ensure that the transaction meets the customer's suitability needs. The claim that the security is a suitable investment must be supported by complete and accurate information obtained from the customer for that purpose, and information provided by the issuer. MSRB G-19 also addresses suitability issues concerning discretionary accounts, and requires that the investment be suitable in such accounts. Finally, G-19 expressly forbids churning in accounts through multiple transactions, or unreasonably large transactions to provide larger commissions to the registered person.

NASD Conduct Rule

NASD Rule 2830 Investment Company Securities
NASD Rule 2830 provides for the regulation of securities of companies that are registered under the Investment Company Act of 1940. The rule provides for the definition of a number of key terms, as follow:
"Brokerage commission" shall not be limited to commissions on agency transactions but shall include underwriting discounts or concessions and fees paid to members in connection with tender offers.
"Covered account" shall mean (A) any other investment company or other account managed by the investment adviser of such investment company, or (B) any other

account from which brokerage commissions are received or expected as a result of the request or direction of any principal underwriter of such investment company or of any affiliated person of such investment company or of such underwriter, or of any affiliated person of an affiliated person of such investment company.

Prime rate, public offering price, rights of accumulation, service fees, and funds of funds

"Prime rate" shall mean the most preferential interest rate on corporate loans at large U.S. money center commercial banks. "Public offering price" shall mean a public offering price as set forth in the prospectus of the issuing company. "Rights of accumulation" shall mean a scale of reducing sales charges in which the sales charge applicable to the securities being purchased is based upon the aggregate quantity of securities previously purchased or acquired and then owned plus the securities being purchased. "Service fees" shall mean payments by an investment company for personal service and/or the maintenance of shareholder accounts. A "fund of funds" is an investment company that acquires securities issued by any other investment company registered under the Investment Company Act of 1940 in excess of the amounts permitted under the act.

Asset based sales charge, deferred sales charge, and front-end sales charge

An "asset based sales charge" is a sales charge that is deducted from the net assets of an investment company and does not include a service fee. Asset-based sales charges may not exceed 0.75%. A "deferred sales charge" is any amount properly chargeable to sales or promotional expenses that is paid by a shareholder after purchase but before or upon redemption. A "front-end sales charge" is a sales charge that is included in the public offering price of the shares of an investment company. For companies without an asset-based sales charge, the aggregate front-end and deferred sales charges may not exceed 8.5% of the offering price, subject to additional discounts for rights of accumulation, quantity discounts, and service fees. For companies with an asset-based sales charge and which charge service fees, the maximum charge is 6.25% of the amount invested. If service fees are not charged, the maximum charge is 7.25%.

Selling dividends, withholding orders, and a refund of sales charges

"Selling dividends" means stating or implying that the purchase of a given security shortly before an ex-dividend date is advantageous to the purchaser, unless there are specific, clearly described tax advantages to the purchaser. This practice is prohibited under NASD Rule 2830. "Withholding orders," in which a member withholds placing a customer's order for his own profit, is prohibited under the rule. A "refund of sales charges" is required if a security issued by an open-end management company is repurchased by the issuer or the issuer's underwriter or is tendered for redemption within seven business days of the original transaction. The broker or dealer must refund the full dealer concession to the underwriter and the underwriter must pay back to the issuer the underwriter's share of the sales charge.

Restrictions on member compensation for the sale of Investment Company securities

FINRA Rule 2830 provides for certain restrictions and limitations on the circumstances and types of compensation that can be paid to members and associated persons for the sale of investment company securities, as follows:

1. No associated person of a member shall accept any compensation from anyone other than the member with which the person is associated.
2. No member or person associated with a member shall accept any compensation from an offeror in the form of securities.
3. Members are obligated to maintain records of all compensation received by the member or its associated persons and such records shall include the names of the offerors, names of the associated persons, and amounts of cash and non-cash compensation.
4. No member shall accept any cash compensation from an offeror unless it is described in a current prospectus of the investment company.

Securities Act of 1933

As provided by the Securities Exchange Commission (SEC), the two objectives of the Securities Act of 1933 are to (i) "require that investors receive financial and other significant information concerning securities being offered for public sale" and (ii) "prohibit deceit, misrepresentations, and other fraud in the sale of securities." Issuing companies can meet these requirements by registering their securities. Registration requires that a company accurately disclose all relevant information concerning the business, the security being offered, company management, and the company's financial position. Without registration, it would be much more difficult for an investor to obtain all of the relevant information needed to make a sound and informed decision.

Issuer and underwriter

The Securities Act of 1933 defines an *issuer* as "every person who issues or proposes to issue any security." Please bear in mind that person is defined as "an individual, a corporation, a partnership, an association, a joint-stock company, a trust, any unincorporated organization, or a government or political subdivision thereof." The issuer plays a key role in the securities markets because the return to the investor, whether through capital appreciation and dividends on equity securities or through coupon and principal repayments on debt securities, will be dependent upon the financial performance of the issuer. The Securities Act of 1933 defines an *underwriter* as "any person who has purchased from an issuer with a view to, or offers or sells for an issuer with, the distribution of any security." Underwriters are primarily utilized by issuers in the primary distribution of securities. The role of the underwriter is to determine the initial pricing and to coordinate the sale and distribution of the security into the market. Underwriters are often also involved in the preparation of the necessary SEC filings and approvals.

SEC

The Securities Exchange Act of 1934 was responsible for the creation of the Securities and Exchange Commission (SEC). As stated by the SEC, their mission is "to protect investors, maintain fair, orderly, and efficient markets, and facilitate capital formation." The SEC accomplishes these objectives by interpreting federal securities laws in order to issue new rules and amend existing rules. Additionally, the SEC plays a critical role in overseeing the inspection of securities firms, brokers, investment advisers, and ratings agencies as well as private regulatory organizations in the fields of securities, accounting, and auditing. The SEC is also responsible for coordinating the regulation of securities across the federal state and foreign regulatory bodies.

The Securities and Exchange Commission (SEC) is responsible for ensuring that market participants have adequate information with which to make informed investment decisions. Thus, the SEC monitors securities exchanges, brokers and dealers, investment advisers, mutual funds, and other market participants to ensure that they are following the established securities laws. The SEC is responsible for monitoring these market participants within the broad guidelines set forth in securities laws such as the Securities Act of 1933 and the Securities Exchange Act of 1934. In order to properly enforce these broad provisions, the SEC engages in rulemaking to clarify its role in specific circumstances. The SEC enforces these rules through either civil or administrative action. Civil action is appropriate in instances where an individual must return illegally gained profits, while administrative action is more appropriate where the punishment is to be barred from participation in the financial markets.

Section 10 of the Securities Exchange Act of 1934

Section 10 of the Securities Exchange Act of 1934, and specifically Rule 10b-5, state that it shall be unlawful for any person, directly or indirectly, by the use of any means or instrumentality of interstate commerce, or of the mails or of any facility of a national securities exchange,
   i. To employ any device, scheme, or artifice to defraud,
   ii. To make any untrue statement of a material fact or to omit to state a material fact necessary in order to make the statements made, in the light of the circumstances under which they were made, not misleading, or
   iii. To engage in any act, practice, or course of business which operates or would operate as a fraud or deceit upon any person,

In connection with the purchase or sale of any security.
Such activities may include insider trading or omissions or misstatements of material facts.

Legislative protection of investors against the use of manipulative and/or deceptive devices, such as those provided under Section 10 of the Securities Exchange Act of

1934, are critical to ensuring the efficient functioning of capital markets. Without such protections, it is likely that larger, institutional investors and funds would try to take advantage of their informational advantages and economics of scale to gain an advantage over other smaller investors without access to that same information. This would lead to lower participation and increased skepticism among smaller investors. Additionally, without faith in an efficient marketplace, fundamental and technical analysis of securities would not be as reliable because of the manipulation of security prices by others within the market.

Investment Company Act of 1940

The Investment Company Act of 1940 intends to regulate investment companies, as such companies are considered to:

1. Issue securities through interstate commerce, which represent a large portion of all securities offered and traded and the national securities exchanges
2. Invest, reinvest, and trade securities through the national securities exchanges and interstate commerce, which comprises a significant portion of all trading activity
3. Invest and trade in significant portions of securities issued by companies who engage in interstate commerce
4. Act as a potential investment for a substantial part of the national savings, which impacts the national economy and the flow of savings into the capital markets
5. Engage in activities of interstate commerce across a geographically diverse group of stakeholders, which cannot be effectively governed through state regulations

The purpose of the Act is to help regulate such investment companies in order to protect investors.

Investment company
"Investment company" is defined within the Investment Company Act of 1940 to mean any issuer that meets one of the following criteria:

1. Is or holds itself out as being engaged primarily or proposes to engage primarily, in the business of investing, reinvesting, or trading in securities
2. Is engaged or proposes to engage in the business of issuing face-amount certificates of the installment type, or has been engaged in such business and has any such certificate outstanding
3. Is engaged or proposes to engage in the business of investing, reinvesting, owning, holding, or trading in securities, and owns or proposes to acquire investment securities having a value exceeding 40 percent of the value of such issuer's total assets (exclusive of government securities and cash items) on an unconsolidated basis.

The three principal classes of investment companies as provided in the Investment Company Act of 1940 are as follows:

1. Face-amount certificate company: an investment company that is engaged or proposes to engage in the business of issuing face-amount certificates of the installment type, or which has been engaged in such business and has any such certificate outstanding.
2. Unit investment trust: an investment company that (A) is organized under a trust indenture, contract of custodianship or agency, or similar instrument, (B) does not have a Board of Directors, and (C) issues only redeemable securities, each of which represents an undivided interest in a unit of specified securities; but does not include a voting trust.
3. Management company: any investment company other than a face-amount certificate company or a unit investment trust.

Management companies: The Investment Company Act of 1940 provides for four subclassifications of management companies. Management companies can be subclassified as either open-end or closed-end companies and as either diversified or non-diversified companies.

An open-end company is a management company that is offering for sale or has outstanding redeemable securities of which it is the issuer. All management companies not fitting this profile are classified as closed-end companies. Securities of closed-end companies can only be purchased on the secondary market and are not available directly from the issuing company.

Management companies are classified as diversified when the following three conditions are met:

1. At least 75 percent of the company's total assets are comprised of cash, government securities, and securities of other investment companies.
2. Securities from any one issuer do not represent more than 5 percent of the management company's total assets.
3. Any securities held by the management company do not represent more than 10 percent of the outstanding voting securities of a given issuer.

All management companies not meeting these three criteria are considered to be non-diversified.

Exemptions from registration

The Investment Company Act of 1940 provides for five types of companies that are exempt from registration, including:

1. Any company organized or created and having its principal office and place of business in Puerto Rico, the Virgin Islands, or any other possession of the United States. The exemption is not valid if securities of the company are offered to residents of any state other than that in which the company is organized.
2. Any company that has gone through a reorganization in the prior five years if (i) the company was not an investment company at the onset of the

reorganization, (ii) at the conclusion of the reorganization all outstanding securities were owned by creditors, and (iii) 50 percent or more of the outstanding voting securities are owned by no more than 25 persons.
3. Any issuer for which there is an outstanding writing filed with the Commission by the Federal Savings and Loan Insurance Corporation stating that the exemption is consistent with the public interest and the protection of investors.
4. Any wholly owned subsidiary of a face-amount certificate company organized prior to 1940 and subject to the state insurance laws of the state in which it is organized.
5. Any company that is not engaged in the business of issuing redeemable securities.

IRA

An individual retirement account (IRA) is a form of retirement savings account. IRAs are a very popular retirement savings tool as they allow investors the opportunity to save for retirement while reducing taxable income, as deferrals into an IRA are tax-deductible to the investor. Additionally, IRAs allow investors the opportunity to supplement their 401(k) retirement savings with an additional source of tax-deferred retirement savings. Investors are limited to only contributing $18,000 to a 401(k) account in 2016 ($24,000 if age 50 or older), so an IRA allows that investor to invest an additional $5,500 ($6,500 if age 50 or older) on a tax-deferred basis.

Traditional and Roth IRAs

There are 2 different forms of IRAs: traditional IRAs and Roth IRAs. A traditional IRA allows an investor to invest on a tax-deferred basis, receiving the tax deduction for contributions to the account and paying income taxes when distributions are paid from the plan. A Roth IRA also allows investors to invest on a tax-deferred basis, but the investor does not receive a tax deduction for contributions to the plan and instead is able to receive tax-free distributions from the plan.

There are a number of rules and restrictions surrounding the ability of an investor to convert a traditional IRA to a Roth IRA. Because of the favorable tax treatment of withdrawals from Roth IRA accounts, these accounts are only available to investors below certain income limits (for 2016, permitted contributions begin to phase out at $117,000 for singles and $184,000 for married couples and are eliminated at $132,000 for singles and $194,000 for married couples). However, these income limits do not limit one's ability to convert a traditional IRA into a Roth IRA. Any investor can choose to convert a traditional to a Roth IRA, provided that taxes are paid on the full amount of the contribution in the tax year of the contribution. However, future contributions to this new account will still be impacted by the income limits.

The primary difference between a Roth Contributory IRA and a Roth IRA is that the latter can be funded either by a rollover or participant contributions, whereas the former is funded only by participant contributions.

Eligibility requirements, contributions limits, and catch-up provisions: In order to contribute to a traditional IRA, an individual who also participates in a company-sponsored retirement plan must fall below certain income limits (for 2016, permitted contributions begin to phase out at $61,000 for singles and $98,000 for married couples and are eliminated at $71,000 for singles and $118,000 for married couples). The 2016 contribution limit to traditional IRA accounts is $5,500. However, for those investors age 50 and over, the contribution limit is raised to $6,500.

In order to contribute to a Roth IRA, an individual must fall below certain income limits (for 2016, permitted contributions begin to phase out at $117,000 for singles and $184,000 for married couples and are eliminated at $132,000 for singles and $194,000 for married couples). The 2016 contribution limit to Roth IRA accounts is $5,500. However, for those investors age 50 and over, the contribution limit is raised to $6,500.

Rollover

Due to the different tax treatments and circumstances regarding certain retirement accounts, the Internal Revenue Service imposes limitations on the types of accounts that can be rolled into an IRA and the types of accounts into which an IRA balance can be added. A traditional IRA can accept rollover contributions from a number of different types of accounts, including a traditional IRA, SIMPLE, SEP, 457(b), qualified plans such as 401(k), and 403(b) plans. A Roth IRA can accept rollovers from all of the above and can also accept rollovers from Roth IRAs and designated Roth accounts with 401(k) and 403(b) plans.

On the other hand, a traditional IRA account can be rolled into a number of other accounts, including a Roth IRA, a traditional IRA, SEP, 457(b), qualified plans, and 403(b) accounts. While Roth IRAs are able to accept rollovers from a variety of different accounts, they can only be rolled into another Roth IRA account given that they represent after-tax dollars.

Restrictions and/or tax treatments

In both traditional and Roth IRA accounts, distributions to participants before age 59½ are considered to be early distributions and they must pay an additional 10% tax. In a traditional IRA account, the IRS imposes certain minimum, or mandatory, distributions beginning at age 70½. The amount of the minimum distribution is calculated as the account balance as of December 31 of the prior year divided by a factor provided by the IRS Uniform Lifetime Table. Roth IRAs differ in that no minimum or mandatory distributions are required prior to the death of the owner of the account. Upon the death of the account owner, the beneficiary has a number of options with respect to any remaining payments from the plan, including continuing to calculate the required minimum distribution based on the decedent's age, calculating the new required minimum distribution based on his/her own age, and withdrawing the entire remaining balance in a lump sum.

Keogh plan

A Keogh plan allows self-employed individuals to save for retirement on a tax-deferred basis. However, a number of limitations apply to who can participate, how much participants can contribute, and how those contributions, and eventual distributions, are taxed. Much like a 401(k) plan, a Keogh is considered to be a "qualified" plan in that it is covered under Internal Revenue Code Section 401(a). As such, contributions to the plan made by the participant are tax-deductible. Once you begin receiving distributions from the plan, those distributions are taxed as ordinary income just as in other qualified plans. In order to be eligible to participate in a Keogh, you must be self-employed, a small business owner, or a sole proprietor. Working for a company does not preclude you from being eligible, so long as you also meet one of the previously mentioned criteria. Because participants are self-employed, the contribution limits to Keogh plans are higher than for many other qualified plans. Keogh plans limit contributions in a given tax year to 25 percent of your earned income, which is income less expenses arising from your self-employment activities.

SEP

Simplified Employee Pension Plans (SEPs) provide a nice alternative for small businesses and self-employed individuals who may not have the time or resources to adequately establish a traditional qualified retirement plan for employees like a 401(k). SEPs allow the employer to contribute funds to a tax-deferred account on behalf of employees. Unlike other types of plans, however, only the employer may contribute. The maximum contribution an employer can make to the account in any given tax year is 25 percent of an employee's pay. A business of any size may establish a SEP and all employees are eligible to participate. Distributions are treated as ordinary income once paid. These plans are especially attractive to employers as they are easier to adopt, require less administrative burden to operate, and do not impose the same filing requirements as other qualified plans.

SIMPLE

A Savings Incentive Match Plan for Employees (SIMPLE) provides the opportunity for small employers (defined as 100 employees or less) the opportunity to provide a tax-deferred retirement savings tool into which employees can elect to contribute their income and employers must make matching or other contributions. The contributions into a SIMPLE are put into an Individual Retirement Account (IRA) for each employee and the IRAs follow all of the same taxation and distribution restrictions as for a traditional IRA. In 2015 and 2016, employees under age 50 are allowed to contribute up to $12,500 into a SIMPLE and employees age 50 and older are allowed to contribute up to $15,500. Employer contributions must take the form of either a dollar for dollar match up to 3% of the employee's compensation or a nonelective contribution equal to 2% of the employee's compensation.

401(k) plans

A business of any size can choose to offer a 401(k) plan to its employees. These plans allow employees to defer receipt of their income, and therefore taxation on that income, to a later date. The contributions grow tax-deferred and distributions are taxed as ordinary income when received. In 2016, employees under age 50 can contribute up to $18,000 into a 401(k) plan and employees age 50 and older can contribute up to $24,000. Employers may also make matching or nonelective contributions to a 401(k) plan, but such contributions are limited to the lesser of 25% of the employee's income or $53,000.

Restrictions
In tax-qualified plans such as IRAs and 401(k) plans, distributions to participants before age 59½ are considered to be early distributions and the employee must pay an additional 10% tax. Thus, the amount will be subject to both ordinary income taxes and the additional 10% tax on the full amount of the distribution. The IRS also imposes certain minimum, or mandatory, distributions from these accounts beginning at age 70½. The amount of the minimum distribution is calculated as the account balance as of December 31 of the prior year divided by a factor provided by the IRS Uniform Lifetime Table. Roth IRAs differ in that no minimum or mandatory distributions are required prior to the death of the owner of the account. Upon the death of the account owner in a traditional IRA or 401(k) plan account, the beneficiary has a number of options with respect to any remaining payments from the plan, including continuing to calculate the required minimum distribution based on the decedent's age, calculating the new required minimum distribution based on his/her own age, and withdrawing the entire remaining balance in a lump sum.

403(b), 403(b)(7), and 501(c)(3)

A 403(b) plan is utilized by employers who are public educational institutions, churches, or nonprofit organizations exempt under 501(c)(3). A 403(b)(7) plan is a specific subset that provides for individual custodial accounts made up of mutual funds. With each of these types of plans, if anyone is allowed to elect to defer compensation, then all participants must be allowed to defer. Participant deferrals into these plans are tax-deductible and accumulate tax-deferred. Distributions can be taken by participants upon reaching age 59½ or upon ending employment, suffering a hardship, or becoming disabled. Once distributions are taken from the plan, they are taxed as ordinary income. The limitations on elective deferrals are the same as those for a 401(k) plan and may not exceed $17,500. In total, employee and employer contributions to the plan cannot exceed $52,000.

457(b) plans

457 plans may come in one of two types: 457(b) plans and 457(f) plans. The key difference between the two is that 457(b) plans are qualified under the Internal Revenue Code and eligible for favorable tax treatment while 457(f) plans are not.

- 84 -

The only organizations that are permitted to offer 457 plans include state or local governments and tax-exempt 501(c) organizations. As with the other qualified plans, contributions to a 457(b) plan are tax-deductible and grow tax-deferred within the account until the time of distribution, at which time they are taxed as ordinary income. Employer and employee contributions are limited to $17,500 for employees under age 50 and $23,000 for employees age 50 and older.

Defined benefit and defined contribution plans

Defined benefit plans, which were especially popular throughout the last several decades, were arrangements between employers and employees under which the employer agreed to pay the employee a specific benefit, often a percentage of salary based on years of service, to the employee upon a qualifying retirement or termination event. Under such an arrangement, the employer is subject to the investment risk of having to set aside enough funds in order to be able to pay the promised benefits. Over the last several years, employers have trended toward the use of defined contribution plans. Under a defined contribution plan, the employer agrees to make a certain contribution to the employee's retirement account, but at that point it becomes the responsibility of the employee to properly invest those funds to ensure he has enough income to meet his retirement needs. This arrangement provides more flexibility to employees to control their own investments, but also shifts the investment risk away from employers. Employers have also trended toward this defined contribution approach as it greatly simplifies the accounting of such retirement benefits.

ERISA

The Employee Retirement Income Security Act of 1974 (ERISA) was enacted to provide minimum standards for pension plans established by employers. One such minimum standard relates to participation, as ERISA provides that the only employees who can be excluded from participation are those under the age of 21 and those who have not yet completed one full year of service with the employer. The act also provides that benefits must vest for participants upon attainment of normal retirement age, which is the earlier of the plan definition or age 65 with five years of service. The act provides for two possible vesting schedules that can be applied to the employer's contributions under the plan: a five-year cliff schedule, in which the employee's vesting percentage is 0 until the fifth year, or a graded schedule in which the employee vests 20% for each completed year of service.

Funding requirements and fiduciary responsibilities
The Employee Retirement Income Security Act of 1974 (ERISA) was enacted to provide minimum standards for pension plans established by employers. One such minimum standard relates to minimum plan funding levels and states that plans must maintain sufficient asset to meet benefit obligations, as calculated given current interest rate and mortality assumptions. These requirements, and the steps required to bring the funding into compliance, vary depending on a number of plan

and employer-specific characteristics. The act also imposes fiduciary responsibilities on anyone who has discretionary authority or management of the plan or renders fee-for-service investment advice regarding plan assets. These fiduciary responsibilities include a duty of loyalty to plan participants and beneficiaries, a duty of prudence in the management of plan assets, a duty to diversify investments as a risk mitigation tool, a duty to act in accordance with the terms of the plan document, and to avoid entering into certain prohibited transactions.

Rollover and transfer rules

Assets from a qualified plan, such as a 401(k), can be rolled over into a number of other accounts, including a traditional IRA or Roth IRA, a SEP, a 457(b) plan, another employer's 401(k) plan, or a 403(b) plan. These assets cannot, however, be rolled over into a SIMPLE IRA. Assets from a 403(b) or 457(b) plan can also be rolled over into a traditional IRA or Roth IRA, a SEP, another employer's 403(b) or 457(b) plan, or a 401(k) plan. As with qualified plan assets, these assets cannot be rolled over into a SIMPLE IRA. Finally, SEP IRAs and SIMPLE IRAs can be rolled over into a traditional IRA or Roth IRA, another employer's SEP, a 403(b) or 457(b) plan, or a 401(k) plan. However, only a SIMPLE can be rolled over into another employer's SIMPLE.

Section 529 College Savings Plan

A Section 529 College Savings Plan is a valuable tool for parents to invest funds on a tax-preferred basis to be used for the costs of college education. Contributions into the plan are made with after-tax dollars, so the benefit of the plan is not experienced at the time of contribution. However, your contributions grow tax-free and can be invested as you choose to allocate the funds within the options available in your specific plan. The funds can be withdrawn to cover any "qualified higher education expenses," including tuition, room and board, and books and computers. While the contribution limits vary by plan and the state or institution offering the plan, often times the contribution limit is in excess of $200,000. Some Section 529 Plans also offer a "prepaid" option, in which the owner of the account will commit to certain payments over a period of time up until the date at which the child is expected to enter the higher education institution. This option essentially "locks in" college costs and moves the investment risk of the funds back to the sponsoring institution.

Coverdell Education Savings Plan

A Coverdell Education Savings Plan is a type of tax-advantaged investment account to allow parents the opportunity to save for educational expenses. Contributions into the plan are not tax-deductible and are limited to $2,000 per year for a given beneficiary. Additional limits may apply to the contributions that can be made to an account depending upon the Modified Adjusted Gross Income of the individual making the contribution. Amounts in the account grow tax-free and can be withdrawn tax-free as long as they are used for any qualified education expenses at any eligible primary, secondary, or higher education institution. Educational expenses such as books, room and board, and computers are also covered as qualified expenses. Any amounts remaining in the account when the beneficiary of the account reaches age 30 must either be distributed (with gains subject to a 10% penalty) or can be rolled over into the account of another family member.

Section 529 College Savings Plan vs. Coverdell Education Savings Plan

Section 529 College Savings Plans and Coverdell Education Savings Plans function in much the same manner, but also have a number of key differences with respect to the use of the funds and contribution limits. Both types of accounts allow for individuals to make after-tax contributions, which are invested and grow tax-free until the tax-free distribution of the funds for "qualified expenses." This definition of qualified expenses is one source of difference. While the Section 529 plans provide only for the funds to be applied to higher education expenses with qualified colleges, Coverdell accounts can be used to fund elementary and secondary educations. Additionally, Section 529 plans allow for significantly higher contributions, when compared to the $2,000 annual limit on contributions into a Coverdell account, and Section 529 Plans also do not impose income limits on the amount of contributions. If a parent was looking to save money for a private high school education, the Coverdell account would allow them to so do. However, in the case of another parent who is concerned about the rising costs of college education, a prepaid Section 529 Plan would be the best option.

Open-end investment company

Share structure and voting rights of shares
Within an open-end investment company, also known as a mutual fund, there may be a number of different share classes available to investors. While each share class invests in the same pool of underlying securities in the same proportion, there are important differences, especially with respect to fees, among the classes. For instance, Class A shares typically have a front-end sales load that is paid at the time of purchase, while Class B and C shares would typically have a contingent deferred sales load and 12b-1 fees. Class B shares may also eventually convert into Class A shares if held for a long enough period of time. While mutual fund shareholders may maintain voting rights over the mutual fund, shareholders do not have voting rights over each individual security that is held by the fund. Instead, it is up to the fund to vote on these shares.

Board of directors
The board of directors of an open-end investment company, or mutual fund, is tasked under the Investment Company Act of 1940 with overseeing the operations of the fund and ensuring that interests are aligned between the fund, its shareholders, and the fund's investment adviser. In order to ensure this protection of shareholder interests, at least 40 percent of the mutual fund's board of directors

must be comprised of independent directors. Within the board of directors, there are also typically a number of specific subcommittees that govern certain key areas of importance, such as audit, corporate governance, or compensation. Additionally, many fund companies will "pool" boards of directors to reduce costs and to leverage existing knowledge for decisions and servicing issues that are similar throughout a given fund family.

Investment adviser

The investment adviser within an open-end investment company, or mutual fund, is responsible for the research and execution of the strategy that is set forth in the fund's prospectus. While the fund's prospectus contains the objective of the fund and any restricted asset classes or securities in which the fund is not permitted to invest, it is up to the investment adviser to actually execute this strategy and to select the individual securities that will most optimally achieve the fund's stated objective. Typically, this investment adviser is paid a fee for this service that is based on a specified percentage of plan assets and is paid from plan assets. This fee is typically categorized under Annual Fund Operating Expenses and disclosed to investors.

Underwriter (distributor), custodian, and transfer agent

The underwriter (or distributor) within an open-end investment company, or mutual fund, is responsible for selling shares of the fund to investors. Due to the fact that the fund is an open-end investment company, this sale of shares is an ongoing process as sales and redemption of shares must be permitted every day. The custodian of an open-end investment company, often a bank or trust company, is responsible for the safekeeping of the securities and assets of the fund. Additional protection is afforded to the fund's investors by segregating this activity to a third party who can verify the type of quantity of securities held. The transfer agent, which may be the same entity as the custodian, is responsible for keeping records related to all of the fund's various transactions and account balances.

Changing investment objectives and policies, investment advisory agreements, and fees

Within a mutual fund, investors maintain a level of protection in that the investment objectives and policies, investment advisory agreements and fees of an open-end investment company cannot be changed without the consent of the shareholders through a majority vote. This protection is important because investors know that their funds will continue to be invested in accordance with the terms of the prospectus at the time at which they invested. While fund companies and their investment advisers maintain discretion over the specific securities in which they invest, the fund's shareholders are guaranteed that the overall portfolio will retain the exposure as promised in the prospectus. Also, given the importance of fees to a fund's performance, it is critical that the fund company or investment advisory fees cannot be increased without a valid reason as approved by shareholders.

Election of directors

The board of directors of an open-end investment company, or mutual fund, is tasked under the Investment Company Act of 1940 with overseeing the operations of the fund and ensuring that interests are aligned between the fund, its shareholders, and the fund's investment adviser. A mutual fund's board of directors is nominated for board service either by the existing board members or by the fund company or shareholders. However, the Investment Company Act of 1940 imposes a requirement that at least two-thirds of a fund's board of directors must have been nominated by the fund's shareholders. This requirement ensures that the fund's shareholders still maintain the majority control over who is serving on the fund's board and making important decisions regarding the fund's investment adviser, transfer agent, custodian, and daily operations.

Selection of independent auditors

The Investment Advisers Act of 1940 requires an open-end investment company, or mutual fund, to retain an independent auditor to certify any financial statements prior to being filed with the Securities Exchange Commission. The selection of the independent auditors depends upon whether or not the mutual fund has established an Audit Committee comprised entirely of independent directors. If a formal Audit Committee has been established by the mutual fund, then the Audit Committee can select and ratify, and annually reengage, the independent audit firm without requiring any approval from shareholders. If no formal Audit Committee has been established by the mutual fund, then shareholder ratification of the audit firm selected by the board is required. This shareholder ratification is rare as most mutual funds maintain a formal Audit Committee.

Access to professional investment managers and simplified diversification

An open-end investment company, or mutual fund, allows a wide range of investors access to a wide array of investment products and financial tools. Without such access, an investor who wanted to diversify his account across a range of diverse asset classes and styles would need to purchase each individual security. Additionally, each security could only be purchased in whole shares. Thus, the minimum amount of investable assets required to properly diversify a portfolio would be substantial. Thanks to open-end investment companies, which often maintain small minimum initial deposits, an investor can pool his money along with that of other investors and achieve access to partial shares of a number of securities, thus achieving diversification with a much smaller initial investment. Additionally, funds of funds allow investors to pool their money in order to gain access to funds with larger minimum investment requirements, thus providing access to additional investment strategies and asset classes that would otherwise not be available to the average investor.

Safekeeping of portfolio securities

The role of a custodian within an open-end investment company, or mutual fund, is to provide for the safekeeping of the securities and assets of the fund and account for cash inflows and outflows of the mutual fund. Without the existence of this valuable service, an investor would have to monitor each of his individual security holdings along with the record keeping of holdings, trade activity, and cash positions. An investor in a mutual fund not only receives the benefit of the custodian's services with respect to the assets safekeeping and tracking, but also receives the benefit of the mutual fund's board of directors monitoring the custodian to ensure they are carrying out their duties to the best of their ability.

Exchange privileges within families of funds
Many open-end investment companies, or mutual funds, offer exchange privileges to investors to entice them to keep their money within the same family of funds when the investors are looking to reallocate into a different fund. While exchange privileges do not provide relief from realizing any taxable gains upon liquidating the mutual fund holding, they do allow investors to prevent paying, or at least not paying the full amount of, any back-end loads that might otherwise be due at the time of sale. For the mutual fund company, this incentive is attractive because the company would prefer to continue earning management and operating expenses on that investor's funds as opposed to charging him a one-time fee and having him invest those funds with a competitor.

Automatic reinvestment of dividend income and capital gains distributions
Many open-end investment companies, or mutual funds, provide services to investors through which any dividend income and capital gains distributions can be automatically reinvested to purchase additional fractional shares of the fund. Without this service, those dividends and distributions would typically be held in a cash or money market fund and would miss out on the earnings of the fund. At the time when a dividend is paid or capital gains are distributed, the investor's base upon which earnings accrete is reduced, thereby reducing total earnings until those funds are reinvested. Thus, minimizing the time that those funds are "out of the market" will help an investor maximize his total returns. Additionally, fund companies do not charge for this service because it is in their best interest as well to have the investor reinvest those funds back into the fund to not deplete the fund's capital base.

Tax and record-keeping information
Open-end investment companies, or mutual funds, provide an important service to their investors by maintaining detailed transactional and tax data to assist the investors with their own tax reporting. Instead of having to track a sale of each individual security that is bought and sold in the underlying fund, investors only need to track their purchase and sale of shares of the fund. Then the investment company will provide the necessary information about the tax generated on each share based on all of the underlying transactions. For an investor who, instead of utilizing an open-end investment company, chose to construct a diversified portfolio of individual securities, it would be up to that investor to track each purchase's cost basis and the dates of the transaction, each dividend that was paid, and the gains on each sale. Not only would this be extremely time-consuming, but it would also

expose the investor to potential liability from incorrectly record keeping or reporting complex transactions.

<u>Evaluation prior to investing</u>
Management experience and investment policies: One of the most important factors when evaluating open-end investment companies is the evaluation of the fund's management team and experience. On one hand, an investor must look at how long the management team has been in place and if the fund has seen significant turnover in recent years. If so, the investor must consider whether prior returns can be expected to continue given that it was largely a different management team who achieved the fund's past returns. Additionally, an investor can evaluate a management team's success in prior endeavors and with prior funds to determine whether or not they believe them to be capable of successfully executing this investment strategy. A fund's investment policies must also be carefully considered. While the investment objective of the fund states what the fund hopes to achieve, the investment policy and strategy outline the more detailed constraints and objectives of the fund, including any requirements or constraints on asset allocation and the types of securities in which the fund may or may not invest. The investor must determine if the strategy and investment policy is consistent with his or her objectives.

Fees and expenses: Over the past several years there has been an increased focus and scrutiny on the fees and expenses charged by open-end investment companies. A great deal of research has been conducted that has shown that very few actively managed funds outperform their associated index when fees and expenses are considered. Thus, selecting a fund with reasonable fees and expenses is a critical component of the investment decision-making process. Fees can come in varying forms across different funds and different share classes, but some of the most frequent fees faced by investors are sales loads, contingent deferred sales charges, and annual operating expenses. Sales loads and contingent deferred sales charges are applied either at the time of purchase or sale and require an investor to come up with additional funds outside of the amount invested, while annual operating expenses are taken out of invested assets periodically throughout the year in the form of reduced earnings. Fortunately, the Securities Exchange Commission has mandated that detailed information regarding any applicable fees and loads must be provided in each funds' prospectus.

Standardized yield: The standardized yield, or SEC yield, was a formula developed by the Securities Exchange Commission to allow for a more standardized and objective comparison of fixed income open-end investment companies, or mutual funds. The standardized yield looks at the dividends and interest over the past 30 days less the funds expenses as compared to the funds total assets, calculated as the product of the number of shares of the fund outstanding and the maximum public offering price. This measure is widely utilized because of its standardization across funds and its consideration of expenses. That doesn't mean it is without its detractors, however. Many investment professionals feel that this measure is not the most accurate way to predict future yields from bond funds because the standardized yield assumes that all dividends are reinvested and all bonds in the fund are held until maturity. It is this last point that is particularly troublesome to many, as bond funds actively trade their holdings and the underlying securities are rarely held to maturity.

Expense ratio: A fund's expense ratio is calculated as the annual dollar cost of operating the fund (including fees paid to the investment manager, custodian, etc.) divided by the average assets under management. This ratio is then collected from investors' funds by lowering the return credited to their accounts. Over the past several years there has been an increased focus and scrutiny on the fees and expenses charged by open-end investment companies. A great deal of research has been conducted that has shown that very few actively managed funds outperform their associated index when fees and expenses are considered. Thus, selecting a fund with a reasonable expense ratio is a critical component of the investment decision-making process.

Quantitative risk management

Many open-end investment companies, or mutual funds, use a quantitative risk management strategy to mitigate a portion of the downside risk that is inherent in the fund's investment strategy. To achieve this risk mitigation, funds will purchase certain derivatives and option contracts that are meant to protect the firm from unexpected negative results. There is, however, a cost to such risk mitigation that may also lower expected returns in positive markets. Thus, an investor must not only be comfortable with the investment strategy of the fund, but also with the risk management strategy employed by the fund. An overly aggressive strategy risk management strategy would be one in which the fund either does not protect against downside risk to the same extent as its peers or one in which unnecessary additional risks are taken through exposure to the derivatives and options. An overly conservative strategy is one in which the fund purchases too much protection from downside risk at the expense of significantly reduced earnings in all types of market cycles.

Reporting mutual fund gain/loss to the IRS and state tax agencies

It is the responsibility of the shareholder, not the fund company or issuing company of a security, to report mutual fund gains and losses to the Internal Revenue Service. A broker, through which the individual investor purchased the fund, will typically provide a Form 1099-DIV, which will report all ordinary, qualified, and tax-exempt dividends received, capital gains distributions, investment expenses, and federal and state income tax withheld. If an investor fails to file this tax return and does not pay taxes on the gain within and distributions from the mutual fund, the Internal Revenue Service may impose a number of sanctions on that investor, including charging you penalties and interest from the date on which the tax would have been due. Investors who mistakenly forget to include this income may have the opportunity to file an amended tax return if the error is discovered prior to it being

92

discovered by the IRS. It is important to remember that a copy of the 1099 is also sent to the IRS, so they will detect that this income is missing from an individual's return.

Calculation of net capital gains/losses for an individual mutual fund investor

The net capital gains (or losses) of a mutual fund are calculated as the income realized from the sale of a fund's underlying investments, plus income from dividends, plus interest income and less the fund's operating expenses. Net capital gains (or losses) may be classified as either realized or unrealized. Realized net capital gains occur from the actual sale of investments and dividend and interest income received, whereas unrealized capital gains occur from the capital appreciation of underlying securities held by the fund. Unrealized gains and losses do not factor into the calculation of net capital gains and losses that impact the taxability of distributions to investors. Instead, the unrealized gains and losses impact the growth of the net asset value of the mutual fund.

Tax treatment of realized and unrealized net capital gains/losses

Realized net capital gains occur from the actual sale of investments and dividend and interest income received, whereas unrealized capital gains occur from the capital appreciation of underlying securities held by the fund. As a regulated investment company, mutual funds are required to distribute all realized net capital gains to their shareholders. These gains are taxable to investors when the distributions are made. Unrealized gains, on the other hand, are not taxable to investors until the gains are actually realized. This may happen in one of two ways. First, the fund may sell certain underlying securities, thereby converting unrealized net capital gains to realized net capital gains. Additionally, unrealized gains will impact the current net asset value of the fund, so an investor may sell his shares in the fund and realize taxable appreciation in the net asset value of the fund, which includes underlying unrealized gains and losses.

Tax consequences for exchanging shares of one fund for another

While some investors may think, based on the name of the transaction, that exchanging shares of one mutual fund for shares of another mutual fund within the same family, that the transaction provides some type of favorable tax treatment, this is not in fact the case. When mutual funds are exchanged, the investor is taxed in just the same way as if the investor had sold shares in the first fund and purchased new shares in the second fund. The benefit of a mutual fund exchange is twofold. First, the exchange operates as a singular transaction to the customer instead of separate transactions for a purchase and a sale. Additionally, the fund company may offer benefits for the investor, including reduced or waived sales or transactions fees, as compared to paying new front-end loads with a new purchase. This mechanism was designed to incent and for the investor to keep his money with the same fund company even when changing his investment objectives.

Calculation of mutual fund investor's tax basis

A mutual fund investor's tax basis is calculated as the purchase price of the fund, plus any fees or commissions paid at the time of the purchase, plus any dividends or capital gains distributions that were reinvested. The tax basis ultimately determines the growth of the net asset value at the time of the sale, which will be taxable to the investor. Upon the exchange of a fund, the investor will be taxed just as if the fund was being sold and a new fund purchased. Thus, the taxable income is equal to the growth in the net asset value above the tax basis. Upon receipt of mutual fund shares through inheritance, the tax basis is equal to their fair market value on the date of the death of the decedent. Upon receipt of mutual fund shares through a gift, the original basis will carry through to the new owner, but may be adjusted for gift taxes paid at the time of gift.

Variable annuities

Accumulation period and annuitization period
Variable annuities are a form of insurance contract that provide for payment of income to the owner of the contract that depends upon the growth of a portfolio of separate account investments. Variable annuities have two distinct phases the accumulation period and the annuitization period. During the accumulation period, the contract owner may make contributions to the contract. The funds invested will grow tax-deferred at a rate determined by the performance of the separate account investments, less the charges imposed by the company that issued the contract. At the end of the accumulation period, the contract is annuitized, meaning that the funds are converted into payments for the remaining life of the contract, which may be either a specified number of years or, in the case of a life annuity, for the remaining life of the contract owner. Within a variable annuity, the funds continue to remain invested in separate accounts and the payments from the plan are typically calculated as the balance divided by a factor determined by the number of payments remaining.

Taxation of payments
One of the primary benefits to a variable annuity is the tax-deferral of growth within the contract during the accumulation phase. However, it is important to also understand the tax consequences once the policy begins to make distributions. There are two methods under which the taxability of variable annuity payments can be calculated: the Simplified Method and the General Rule. The Simplified Method allows an investor to calculate the tax free recovery of cost in each payment as the total cost divided by the number of anticipated payments. Thus, the Simplified Method provides for a constant dollar amount of cost recovery in each payment, until such cost has been fully recovered. The General Rule, on the other hand, calculates the tax-free cost recovery as the total cost divided by the expected total return, which is defined to be the total expected payments provided by the contract.

Tax treatment and penalties for the surrender, death benefit, or Section 1035 exchange

When a variable annuity contract is surrendered, the amount received is taxable to the extent that it exceeds the tax basis. Additionally, a surrender or withdrawal of policy values prior to age 59½ may trigger an additional excise tax for early withdrawal of the funds.

If the owner of a variable annuity dies before receiving all payments, the lump-sum payment to the decedent's beneficiary will be taxable to the extent it exceeds the amount of cost basis that had not yet been withdrawn from the contract through payments.

Internal Revenue Code Section 1035 allows the owner of a variable annuity contract to execute a tax-free exchange of their contract for a new variable annuity contract. While the transaction will not be taxable, there may be inherent contract charges applicable to such an exchange.

Variable life insurance

Tax treatment of premium payments, cash value growth, and death benefits

Premium payments into a life insurance policy are not tax-deductible to the policy owner. This is in contrast to contributions to a number of other retirement savings vehicles, such as an Individual Retirement Account, in which contributions can be deducted, which is thought to increase the savings incentive. One of the most attractive features of a variable life insurance policy is that all cash value growth within the policy is tax free, if the policy is held until maturity. Thus, so long as the policy owner holds the policy until death proceeds are received, no tax will be due. However, if the policy owner decides to surrender the policy, then the cash value will be taxable to the extent it exceeds the tax basis. Another benefit of a variable life insurance policy is that any withdrawals will come first from basis, which provides a good source of tax-free liquidity. The death benefits received from a variable life insurance policy are tax-free to the beneficiary.

Tax treatment upon surrender of the policy or upon a Section 1035 exchange

One of the most attractive features of a variable life insurance policy is that all cash value growth within the policy is tax-free, if the policy is held until maturity. However, if the policy owner decides to surrender the policy, then the cash value will be taxable to the extent it exceeds the tax basis. Any partial withdrawals from a variable life insurance policy will come first from any available cost basis, which provides the policy owner with a good source of tax-free liquidity. Internal Revenue Code Section 1035 allows the owner of a life insurance policy to execute a tax-free exchange of their contract for either a new variable life insurance policy or a variable annuity contract. While the transaction will not be taxable, there may be inherent contract charges applicable to such an exchange.

UIT

A unit investment trust (UIT) is one of three types of investment companies, in addition to closed-end funds and open-end funds, or mutual funds. Units are issued at the inception of the UIT and are capitalized with the proceeds from that initial issuance. Perhaps the most distinguishing characteristic of unit investment trusts is the extremely low turnover in the investment portfolio. Contrary to mutual funds and closed-end funds, the initial securities purchased in the UIT are typically held through the maturity of the UIT. Consequently, a UIT does not have an investment adviser or board of directors like mutual funds. Additionally, UITs will establish a termination date at their inception, and at that point the UIT will cease to exist and all units will be redeemed.

Value and price
Unit investment trusts (UITs) are valued and priced in much the same way as their mutual fund counterparts. Due to the limited number of securities in UITs and the lower turnover, pricing of UITs requires significantly less administrative effort on the part of the UIT than with mutual funds. The net asset value of the UIT is simply the total of all underlying securities divided by the number of units that are currently outstanding. However, unlike mutual funds, the growth of assets within Unit Investment Trusts experiences much less drag as a result of investment management fees that come along with more active management and hiring an adviser as well as taxes on the early sale of securities and higher portfolio turnover.

Trading on secondary markets and restrictions on redeeming shares
Unit investment trusts (UIT) are issued only at the inception of the fund. However, units are redeemable at any time upon request by an investor and must be redeemed by the trust upon receiving that request at the net asset value at that time. In order to promote keeping the funds invested as investors redeem shares, many sponsors of UITs will maintain a secondary market for units of UITs for investors to be able to both buy and sell their units to the sponsor. Contrary to mutual funds, in which a single share or even a portion of a single share can be redeemed, only large blocks of units can be redeemed within UITs.

Closed-end fund

Closed-end funds, or closed-end companies, are one of three types of investment companies, in addition to open-end investment companies, or mutual funds, and unit investment trusts (UITs). Closed-end funds are distributed to the public through an initial public offering of a given number of shares, which are then traded in the secondary market. Due to the fact that these securities are traded in the secondary market and bought and sold between investors, the price paid for these securities may differ from the net asset value of the fund. Unlike mutual funds and unit investment trusts (UITs), sponsors of closed-end funds are not required to redeem investors' shares. As a result, closed-end funds are also able to invest in much more illiquid securities.

Value and price

Just as with open-end funds, or mutual funds, and unit investment trusts (UITs), closed-end funds have a net asset value that is calculated as the value of all underlying assets divided by the number of shares that were issued. Due to the fact that these securities are traded in the secondary market and bought and sold between investors, the price paid for these securities may differ from the net asset value of the fund. The price may track closely to the net asset value, but will ultimately be determined by supply of and demand for shares in the secondary market. Additionally, the sponsor of a closed-end fund may specify certain intervals at which to accept redemptions from investors.

Insurance company separate account

As provided in Section 2(a)(37) of the Investment Company Act of 1940, an insurance company separate account means "an account established and maintained by an insurance company pursuant to the laws of any State or territory of the United States, or of Canada or any province thereof, under which income, gains and losses, whether or not realized, from assets allocated to such account, are, in accordance with the applicable contract, credited to or charged against such account without regard to other income, gains or losses of the insurance company." This separate account differs from the insurer's general account, which does take into account the income, gains, or losses of the insurance company as a whole.

3a-8 of the Securities Act of 1933

Section 3a-8 of the Securities Act of 1933 states that the following are exempt from registration under the Act, "Any insurance or endowment policy or annuity contract or optional annuity contract, issued by a corporation subject to the supervision of the insurance commissioner, bank commissioner, or any agency or officer performing like functions, of any State or Territory of the United States or the District of Columbia." The reason that these securities are exempt from registration is because these securities already fall under the jurisdiction of insurance commissioners and other regulatory bodies and the burden placed onto insurance companies of having to also register these securities with the SEC would be overly burdensome. By making the separate accounts and general accounts exempt from the SEC, the government can avoid duplicate regulation.

Investment risk

The 10 types of investment risk are business risk, credit risk, interest rate risk, purchasing power risk, liquidity risk, reinvestment risk, taxability risk, market risk, social/political risk, and currency exchange risk. When evaluating potential investments, each of these risks must be considered in order to determine the comprehensive level of risk of the investment. Without a comprehensive understanding of the risks of the investment, an investor or adviser cannot ensure that any investment recommendation is truly suitable. While it is important to consider the return characteristics of an investment, solely relying upon expected return provides an incomplete analysis of potential investments because any of the 10 previously mentioned risks could positively or negatively impact the return or the benefit of a given investment. For instance, if an investor requires liquidity in five years, it will do him no good to invest in a hedge fund that earns 20% annually but locks up his funds for at least 10 years. As another example, a foreign company may have tremendous growth prospects, but currency fluctuations could negate an investor's gains in the security when converted back to the investor's home currency.

Business risk

Business risk is defined as the possibility that a company's financial performance could have a negative impact on the returns to the company's investors. Business risk can be influenced by a number of factors, including sales/revenue that don't meet expectations, shrinking margins, or increased pressure from competitors. As one example, assume Company A's common stock is currently valued at $45 per share and analysts' expectations assume $500 million of revenue in the most recent quarter. Company A then reports quarterly revenue of only $350 million, causing the stock price to fall and resulting in capital losses for investors. Business risk is applicable to fixed income securities as well, given that the company's financial performance will impact the coupon rate on future fixed income issues. As the company issues higher coupon securities, the value of the older, lower coupon debt instruments will fall.

Credit risk

Credit risk is defined as the possibility that a company may not live up to its contractual obligations. Credit risk is most commonly associated with fixed income investments as the company must provide for periodic coupon payments within fixed income investments and these coupon payments represent a large portion of the overall return provided. Typically, companies with financial difficulties who may not be able, or willing, to meet coupon payments must issue debt instruments with significantly higher coupon rates to compensate investors for taking that additional risk. While equity investments are not typically subject to the same level of credit risk, the value of an equity investment in a company who fails to make coupon payments and defaults on its debt instruments will fall significantly.

Interest rate risk

Interest rate risk is defined as the possibility that a change in market interest rates or in the term structure of interest rates or yield curve could have a negative impact on an investor's returns. Like credit risk, interest rate risk is primarily associated with fixed income investments. As market interest rates rise, the price of a fixed income security will fall because the investor's preference, at equal prices, would be to receive the security with the higher coupon rate. In order to compensate investors and to equate the value of the two securities, the price of the lower coupon rate security must decrease, thus increasing the yield of the security to bring it back into balance. For equity securities, a rise in market interest rates would typically result in a slight decrease in the price of securities since the risk-free return would now be higher and the return on equity must also rise as a result.

Purchasing power risk

Purchasing power risk is defined as the risk faced by investors that unexpected changes in inflation rates can negatively impact the return of an investment. Equity investors do not face much purchasing power risk because unexpected changes in inflation should result in an increase in dividend rates as well as appreciation of the stock's price. However, once a fixed income investment is purchased, the payments they receive are fixed. As inflation rises at a rate greater than what was expected when the security was purchased, those fixed payments become less valuable than expected. Additionally, when inflation rates rise, the nominal market interest rates will also rise, which will negatively impact the price of fixed income securities.

Liquidity risk

Liquidity risk is defined as the possibility that the lack of liquidity within a security can have a negative impact for investors. One characteristic common to low liquidity is a wide spread between bid and ask prices. As investors who are forced to sell their positions receive lower prices due to the spread, those investors who are still holding their positions now see lower valuations. Liquidity risk is more relevant to equity investors than to fixed income investors, as fixed income investors are at least entitled to receive coupon payments and principal repayment at the scheduled maturity of the security. However, equity securities have no scheduled maturity and the only way for an investor to realize earnings on an equity investment is to sell that position.

Reinvestment risk

Reinvestment risk is defined as the possibility that investors who receive cash flows from securities will be forced to reinvest those cash flows into securities with lower interest rates or to accept additional risk in order to receive an equivalent rate. One example of reinvestment risk is an investor who purchases an 8% coupon, 20-year bond. Five years following the investment, the yield curve has flattened such that the long-end of the curve is now lower than it had previously been. As coupon payments are received every six months, the investor must now invest those coupons at a lower rate. This will impact the investor's yield to maturity, which assumes that each cash flow is reinvested at the original rate.

Taxability risk

Taxability risk is defined as the possibility that an investment's return will be negatively impacted because of a change in the tax treatment of the investment's earnings. Returns on equity investments are impacted by prevailing tax rates on dividends and short- and long-term capital gains, while fixed income coupons may be taxable or may be tax-exempt, depending on the issuer. An equity investor could be subject to taxability risk if he purchased a small-cap growth security that he plans to hold for five years. The expected pre-tax return on the security is 10% and the long-term capital gains tax rate is 18%, so the expected after-tax return is 8.2%. Now consider a change in legislation that would increase the tax rate to 25%. The investor's expected after-tax return has fallen to 7.5%, which would likely reduce the share price of the stock. Alternatively, consider an investor who purchased a tax-exempt fixed income security. With new legislation that would eliminate the preferential tax treatment, the after-tax yield would immediately fall. In order to bring the yield back to market rates, the price of the security would fall.

Market risk

Market risk is defined as a source of non-diversifiable risk that would be expected to negatively impact the returns on all securities. Some examples of systemic or market risks include terrorist attacks, natural disasters, and bank runs. These risks cannot be controlled by the security's issuing company and will impact all of their competitors. Equity securities were significantly impacted following the terrorist attacks on 9/11. None of the issuing companies could have done anything to prevent this decline in share prices and investors could not have diversified away from this risk as it impacted securities throughout the entire market. While it would be intuitive to assume that such an event would also negatively impact returns on equity investments, the opposite can often be true. As equity prices fall and investors look for safer alternatives, the demand for fixed income securities rises, increasing prices and driving down rates similar to what we've seen in the markets over the last several years since the financial turmoil of 2008 and 2009.

Social/political risk

Social/political risk is defined as the possibility that changes in the governmental structure of a country or an unsettling of the political landscape could negatively impact the returns on both equity and fixed income investments. Typically, both equity and fixed income investments would be impacted similarly by social/political risk. For instance, assume an investor has purchased both equity and fixed income securities that were issued by a company in Country A. A year later, a new political faction wins the election and implements policies to limit free enterprise and reduce transparency to the rest of the world. With this new political structure in place, Country A is now a much less attractive place to invest in, and the investor will see the share price of the equity fall and the interest rate on future debt issuances rise. New investors will demand a higher return (achieved through lower current prices) to compensate them for this higher level of political risk and uncertainty. This risk is much more prevalent in emerging markets with less stable political structures.

Currency exchange risk

Currency exchange risk is defined as the possibility that fluctuations in exchange rates will negatively impact an investor's return on a foreign equity or fixed income investment when translated back to home currency terms. An equity investor from the United States who makes an investment in an equity security of a Chinese firm must consider not only the return that the company will generate, but how fluctuations in the exchange rate will increase or decrease that return over time. For instance, assume that the investor makes a $10,000 investment in the Chinese equity security. Three years later, the investor has earned a 20% return in local currency terms but when he sells the position and needs to convert the yuan back to dollars, the dollar has appreciated 25% against the yuan. As a result, the investor only receives back $9,600 for a 4% loss.

Diversification

Over the past several years, diversification has come to the forefront of investor education as a fundamental principle of wise investing. Nearly everyone is familiar with the phrase "don't put all of your eggs in one basket." Those who would advocate for diversification would make a similar argument. By investing in several different securities, investors are able to minimize expected risk as measured by the standard deviation of expected returns while maintaining the same level of expected return. When an investor places all of her money within one security, she is exposed to a higher concentration of risk as one failed product, earnings underperformance, or shift in the competitive landscape of that company's industry could jeopardize her entire investment. However, by diversifying into two securities, only half of her investment would be subject to the risk of an occurrence with that company, while the other half of her funds would be subject to the risks of a different company. The more distinct the two investments are from each other (lower correlation of returns), the greater the benefit of diversification is expected to be.

Diminishing marginal benefit

Diversification is a method of reducing risk for a given level of expected return by investing across a number of securities. The benefits of diversification, however, diminish as more and more securities are added to the portfolio and an investor must weigh the benefits of diversification across a large number of securities with the resources necessary to follow that many securities. The diminishing marginal benefit can be seen in the following example: Suppose an investor is currently holding one equity security, Fund A. The investor's financial adviser tells the investor he needs to diversify and the investor liquidates half his position in Fund A and purchases Fund B. The investor has just substantially reduced his risk by adding one additional security to his portfolio. A second investor's portfolio is comprised of 50 different equity securities. He adds one more security to make the total 51. While this second investor is now more diversified, the marginal benefit of the first investor adding an additional fund to his portfolio far outweighs that of the second investor.

Impact of increase in market interest rates

An increase in interest rates would result in a decrease in price of a debt security. Future cash flows expected from the debt security would be discounted back to the present date at a higher rate, making the security less valuable compared to other alternatives now available in the marketplace. An increase in interest rates would have no impact on the par value of a debt security. The par value of a debt security is set at the date of issue and does not change over the life of the security. An increase in market interest rates would decrease the duration of a debt security, which is a measure of the average time to receive all cash flows from a debt security. Because an increase in market interest rates represents an increase in the discount rate applied to future cash flows, the increase has the effect of weighting the duration more toward near-term cash flows and decreasing the duration. An increase in market interest rates would decrease the premium or increase the discount of a debt security. The premium/discount is the difference between the current price of the debt security and the par value of the security. Thus, as the price falls with a rise in rates, the premium or discount also changes accordingly.

An increase in market interest rates would increase the current yield of a security, which is defined as the annual interest payments divided by the current price. With the increase in market rates, the price of the security decreases, thus increasing current yield. An increase in interest rates would have no impact on the nominal yield of a debt security, which is also known as the coupon rate. The nominal yield is determined at the issuance of a debt security and does not change from issuance to maturity. An increase in market interest rates would increase the yield to maturity of a debt security, which is defined as the rate at which the discounted coupon payments and principal repayments equal the price of the security. As rates rise, the price of the debt security falls. In order to maintain the equivalence between the discounted cash flows and the falling price, the yield to maturity must rise, which reduces the value of the discounted cash flows back to the lower price.

Role of inflation in price of equity and debt securities

For equity securities, inflation can have varying degrees of impact on valuations depending upon the ability of the issuing company to pass through rising costs to customers through increased prices. If companies are able to pass through all of the increasing costs to customers, then increases in inflation should not have a material impact on the price of the equity securities because the underlying financials and margins will remain essentially unchanged. For debt securities, unexpected changes in inflation levels can have a significant impact in valuations. When a debt security is issued, market interest rates consist of the real rate and an adjustment for inflation. Thus, an increase in inflation would increase market interest rates, which reduces the value of a previously issued debt security.

Federal Reserve and monetary policy

The role of the Federal Reserve is to set monetary policy by impacting the money supply and credit available to banks, which in turn influences the market interest rates. The goal of the Federal Reserve is to manage the interest rates and achieve a balance between rates that are too high, which would stifle economic growth and lead to higher unemployment, and rates that are too low, which would lead to economic growth that is too rapid and would eventually lead to an overheated economy and rapid inflation. One tool that is used by the Federal Reserve is open-market operations, in which the Federal Reserve buys and sells US treasuries in order to influence the amount of reserves in the banking system, which impacts interest rates and credit availability. Another tool that the Federal Reserve can employ is setting the discount rate, which drives market interest rates. Perhaps even more importantly than its impact on market rates, the discount rate and the announcements regarding rates are the most visible announcement by the Fed to the markets about their views on the future of the economy and their future plans.

Impact of monetary policy on securities

An appropriate monetary policy is critically important in allowing debt and equity securities to achieve their maximum potential values. A monetary policy that is too expansionary, with extremely low rates and a huge supply of credit, will lead to increased equity prices and increased prices of debt securities as currently issued securities will have significantly lower interest rates. While everyone loves increasing security prices, the Federal Reserve must be careful to not hold rates for too long or else the rising prices may turn into a bubble and an overheated economy. In the instance of a tightening monetary policy, equity and debt prices will contract. Equity prices will contract as interest rates rise, companies will not take additional leverage to finance new projects, and their financial performance will struggle. Additionally, debt security prices will fall because market interest rates are higher and investors will require a more discounted price of the security.

Fiscal policy

The House of Representatives, Senate, and President are all responsible for enacting the fiscal policy of the United States. The primary tools that the government can use to enact fiscal policy include changing taxes, interest rates, and government spending. By increasing taxes, the US government can contract the growth of the economy and displace private spending with government spending. The degree to which taxes slow the growth of the economy is dependent both upon the method in which the taxes are levied (how much and upon who), as well as how that additional revenue is spent by the government, which is another tool of the government in setting fiscal policy. Certain projects, such as building infrastructure, stimulate the economy by creating jobs and encouraging new business formation, and can actually work to stimulate certain parts of the economy, while other spending on certain entitlements and meeting basic human needs will not stimulate the economy.

Fiscal policy impacts the performance of securities, both debt and equity, by impacting corporate performance as well as influencing expectations about future economic performance. For instance, an expansionary fiscal policy, which could be implemented through a reduction in personal income taxes, would likely stimulate consumer spending, thus driving up corporate revenues and increasing equity valuations. If a company is valued at a given price-earnings ratio, then as earnings increase, equity prices should also increase accordingly. Along the same lines, those same companies' costs of debt should decrease as they will be more likely to meet their obligations and their likelihood of default will be reduced. In the face of contractionary fiscal policy, such as would occur in the case of an increase in personal income taxes, personal spending would likely fall, thus reducing corporate earnings and decreasing equity valuations. Also, falling revenues would increase the likelihood of default of debt, thus increasing the cost of debt and reducing the value of the existing debt securities.

Open, Maintain, Transfer, and Close Accounts, and Retain Appropriate Account Records

Individual registration and joint tenants with rights of survivorship

An individual registration ownership of mutual fund shares means that there is only one individual owner and beneficial recipient of the securities in the account. Only this individual may authorize transactions on behalf of the account. When the owner of the account dies, the owner's will dictates the distribution of the account's assets. If no will exists, state and federal laws dictating estate distribution and beneficiaries will dictate the distributions. The other most common form of ownership for mutual fund shares is joint tenants with rights of survivorship. In this instance, the account has 2 or more owners who all share equally in the gains and losses of the account. Upon the death of one account owner, that portion is redistributed equally among all remaining owners.

Tenants in common

Tenants in common is another form of mutual fund account ownership (in addition to joint tenants with rights of survivorship); however, these two forms differ from each other in a number of key features. For instance, whereas the account is owned in equal proportions by each owner within the joint tenants with rights of survivorship, the account can be divided into specific ownership proportions under tenants in common. The ownership proportions will determine the allocation of income among owners. Another key difference between these two joint ownership structures relates to the treatment of the account upon the death of one of the account owners. Under joint tenants with rights of survivorship, that portion of the account attributable to the owner who died is equally shared among the remaining owners. Under tenants in common, the deceased owner's portion of the account is passed to whoever is named in the deceased's will as a beneficiary.

UGMA account

The acronym UGMA stands for a Uniform Gift to Minors Account. UGMA accounts allow adults to open and manage a trade account for the benefit of an underage individual. The adult who manages the UGMA is called a custodian. All assets within a UGMA are held in the custodian's name until the minor reaches the age of majority. The age of majority depends on the laws of each state. The custodian of the account has full rights over that account until the minor reaches the age of majority. A custodian may manage several accounts and a minor may be the principal in multiple accounts. However, any single account can have only one custodian and one minor. The custodian has a fiduciary responsibility to ensure the account is maintained properly for the benefit of the minor.

Account authorizations

One means of account authorization is power of attorney (POA), where the authority to represent someone in legal, private, or business matters is held by another person; these must be formalized in writing.

-Another means is by corporate resolution, where a corporation as a unit performs some action. This is usually accomplished with a legal document, voted upon by the corporation's board of directors.

-Trading authorization can serve as a lesser substitute for power of attorney. There are different degrees of trading authorization, where the client grants a level of power to a broker (or some other agent) for the trading of his securities. This is less than the authorization granted in power of attorney, since it applies only to trading (and only to the trading that the client specifies).

-Discretionary accounts are accounts where a broker is authorized to make securities transactions on the client's behalf without the client's consent. These require the signing of a discretionary disclosure for written confirmation.

SEC Rule 17a-3

Memorandum of each brokerage order given or received for the purchase or sale of securities (for customer and firm accounts) - whether executed or unexecuted. The memorandum is to show the terms and conditions; the account for which entered; the time the order was received; the time of entry; the price it was executed; the identity of any associated persons responsible for the account; the identity of the person who entered or accepted the order; and the time of execution or cancellation.

Memorandum of each purchase and sale for the account of the firm - including the price, the time of execution, and if the transaction was with a customer other than a broker or dealer, a memorandum of each order received showing the time of receipt, the terms and conditions; the identity of each associated person responsible for the account; and the identity of the person who entered or accepted the order.

ACATS

The Automated Customer Account Transfer Service allows broker/dealers to transfer funds and securities to other broker/dealers electronically. The receiving firm will provide an ACAT form to the sending firm that requests the funds and/or securities. The holding firm must respond to the request in one business day after they receive the request. They must fulfill the request unless the account does not contain transferable assets, the customer's social is incorrect, the registration of the account requested does not match their records, or there is no signature (or an irregular customer signature) on the form. If the form is rejected, action must be taken by the applicable firm within 5 business days. After the holding firm approves the form, they must freeze the account and cancel all orders excluding options. The holding firm then has three days to transfer the account to the receiving firm. ACATS transfers are not exclusive to full transfers; partial account transfers may be accomplished with ACATS.

FINRA rules 5230, 2251, and 2267

Payments involving publications that influence the market price of a security (FINRA Rule 5230) - a member is not to give anything of value to a person in order to influence or reward an action related to a publication or other media.

Forwarding of proxy and other materials (FINRA Rule 2251) - a member is to forward promptly all information required by this Rule and the SEC regarding a security to its beneficial owner if the name of registration is different than the name of the beneficial owner.

Investor education and protection (FINRA Rule 2267) - a member is to annually provide in writing to every customer the FINRA BrokerCheck Hotline number, the FINRA web-site address, and a statement informing the customer of an available BrokerCheck brochure.

Customer account transfer contracts

Customers who wish to transfer securities from one FINRA member to another may submit an automated customer account transfer form, or ACAT. Per FINRA Rule 11870, each FINRA member must "expedite and coordinate activities" to comply with the customer's request. Rule 11870 also provides for non-ACAT transfers via non-ACAT forms. ACAT forms will vary from member to member, but will generally contain the same information. The member that receives the instructions must validate (declare valid) the request or claim that the request is not valid (take issue) within one business day. After that, they must act in a reasonably speedy manner to facilitate the request. If the ACAT requests that the securities be liquidated first, it will generally take longer to process.

Discretionary accounts

Excessive transactions - when a member has discretionary powers over the account of a customer, the member may not transact purchases or sales that are in excessive size or frequency in comparison to the size and character of the account.

Authorization and acceptance of account - a member may not exercise its own discretion in a customer's account unless they have received written authorization from the customer.
Approval and review of transactions - a member shall quickly and in writing approve all discretionary transactions and regularly review all discretionary accounts to prevent any excessive transactions.

Exceptions - the Rule does not apply to the time and price that an order received from the customer is executed at, though such orders are only valid through the end of the business day. It also does not apply to certain bulk exchanges of net asset value of money market mutual funds.

Records to be preserved by certain exchange members

Records to be preserved by certain exchange members, brokers and dealers (Rule 17a-4) - every broker and dealer is to keep general records for six years. For the first two years of record retention, the records are to be kept in an easily accessible place. Records of associated persons are to be kept until three years after the person's employment has terminated. Records can be produced or reproduced on micrographic media. If records are to be maintained by an outside service bureau, such bureau is to file with the Commission.

Rule 17a-8 of the Securities Exchange Act of 1934

Under Rule 17a-8 of the Securities Exchange Act of 1934, brokers and dealers are required to comply with the reporting, record keeping, and record retention requirements set forth by the Bank Secrecy Act, the goal of which is to prevent and detect money laundering and other illegal financial activities. One such requirement of the Bank Secrecy Act is that brokers and dealers must implement Customer Information Programs that are designed to verify the identity of their customers, collect and maintaining information necessary to identify their customers, and determine whether customers appear on any government published lists of known or suspected terrorist organizations. Additionally, brokers and dealers ought to follow the training programs for educating employees on how to identify suspicious activity in customer's accounts and how to report such suspicious behavior to the proper governmental authorities, such as through Suspicious Activity Reports (SARs).

Regulation S-P (Privacy of Consumer Financial Information)

Regulation S-P (Privacy of Consumer Financial Information) contains at its core three main purposes or functions:
1. The regulation requires financial institutions to notify its customers of its privacy practices
2. The regulation prohibits financial institutions from disclosing nonpublic personal customer information to third parties, unless the institution has disclosed its practices to the customer and the customer has failed to opt out of such disclosure
3. The regulation provides certain industry standards for financial institutions regarding privacy practices and disclosure of customer information.

Through the various components of Regulation S-P, customers of financial institutions are afforded additional protection from the distribution of their personal information, while financial institutions are provided with a "road map" to follow to ensure they are staying in compliance with the regulation.

Disclosure limitations
Regulation S-P (Privacy of Consumer Financial Information) provides for a number of improvements to the required disclosure by financial institutions to their customers regarding the institutions privacy practices and providing of personal customer information to third parties. For example, financial institutions regulated under Regulation S-P must provide disclosure to customers including the nonpublic personal data that is collected, how that data is used, and with whom it can be shared. Additionally, the financial institution must provide the opportunity for its customers to "opt-out," which means that they can choose to prohibit the financial institution from sharing this information with third parties. As technology has spread and become an ever increasingly important component of the financial markets, so too has the concern over privacy laws, identity theft, and the protection of personal information. This is an issue that will continue to play an important role in consumer protection in the years to come.

Exceptions
Regulation S-P (Privacy of Consumer Financial Information) provides for certain exceptions to the disclosure and privacy policies. A good working knowledge of these exceptions is important to avoid confusion or miscommunication around practices that might otherwise be considered violations of the regulation. For instance, the regulation provides that the initial privacy notice must be provided at the beginning of the customer relationship, which is defined to occur at the time of share purchases.

However, this privacy delivery requirement may be delayed if:
1. Providing the notice prior to the customer relationship would delay the customer's transaction and the customer agrees to receive the notice at a later date; or
2. A nonaffiliated broker or dealer creates the customer relationship with the fund without the fund's prior knowledge.

Additionally, there are exceptions to the ability of the customer to opt-out of the sharing of personal nonpublic information, when the institution must share that information with a third party in order to effect transactions on behalf of the customer or servicing a customer's products and accounts.

US Patriot Act

The PATRIOT Act was established for all forms of business following the terrorist attacks of September 11, 2001. The PATRIOT act was established to help businesses, especially financial institutions, prevent funneling of funds to terrorist organizations. The PATRIOT Act requires that financial institutions establish and maintain a customer information program (or CIP). The minimum required information for collection for CIPs consists of the customer's name, address, social security number, and date of birth. Per the requirements of the USA PATRIOT Act, it is the responsibility of the FINRA member opening a new account to confirm that the customer is who they say they are (usually via some form of government issued identification), retain the method used to determine the customer's identity, and ensure that the person is not on the Office of Foreign Assets Control (OFAC) list. The OFAC list contains the names of individuals and organizations with ties to terrorism.

Bank Secrecy Act

The Bank Secrecy Act, also known as the Currency and Foreign Transactions Reporting Act of 1970, serves to assist the United States government in uncovering and preventing illegal financial activities such as money laundering. Under the act, financial institutions in the United States are required to report and to maintain records for all cash transactions occurring in a single day in excess of $10,000. In addition, financial institutions must maintain records on their premises for a period of five years for any cash purchases of monetary or negotiable instruments between $3,000 and $10,000 in a single day. Finally, those financial institutions are also required to report any activity they feel to be suspicious or believe may be part of an attempt to conduct money laundering, tax evasion, fraud, or other illegal activities.

Required information on the sender and recipient of funds

Under the Bank Secrecy Act, which is designed to prevent and detect money laundering and other illegal financial activities, financial institutions are required to collect certain data on the sender and recipient of funds for certain transactions. The information to be retained by the sender's financial institution includes:
1. Name and address of the sender
2. Amount that was sent
3. Execution date of the transaction
4. Payment instructions provided by sender
5. Identity of recipient's financial institution

The information for the recipient includes:
1. Name and address of the recipient
2. Account number of the recipient
3. Any other specific identifiers of the recipient

These requirements are important because they require the financial institutions to gather relevant data that may assist them in uncovering and prevent illegal financial activities. They also create a paper trail that can assist in future investigations, if necessary.

Anti-Money Laundering Compliance Program and the Customer Identification Program

Financial institutions and banks are required to implement Anti-Money Laundering Compliance Programs as part of the Bank Secrecy Act. A number of factors are considered in the development of each institutions compliance program, including the products and services it offers, customer demographics, and geographical locations, among others. Each institution must develop a comprehensive program that determines high risk products or services, establishes monitoring and record-keeping requirements for each line of business, and, finally, provides for a systematic approach to reporting and reviewing any suspicious activity. One component of an effective Anti-Money Laundering Compliance Program is an effective Customer Information Program, under which the financial institution gathers data to ensure that it knows the true identify of each of its customers. The information that they collect on customers includes, at a minimum, the customer's name, date of birth, address, and identification number (such as a Social Security number). The institution must use some current form of identification of the customer to verify this information, such as a driver's license or passport. In the case of an institutional account, incorporation or trust documents may be used.

Suspicious Activity Report

Financial institutions are required to file Suspicious Activity Reports (or SARs) whenever they observe transactions or trends in customer's accounts that lead them to believe that the customer is involved in money laundering, tax evasion, fraud, or other illegal financial activities. These reports help regulators and law enforcement officials to not only pursue and prosecute individual cases, but also to compile data and analyze trends across the entire financial industry. Thus, it is important to have consistency and quality in the information that is provided in the SARs. SARs typically include the following information:
1. Who is conducting the suspicious activity?
2. What instruments or mechanisms are being used to facilitate the suspect's activity?
3. When and where did the suspicious activity take place?
4. Why is the activity in question suspicious?
5. How did the suspicious activity occur?

Obtain, Verify, and Confirm Customer Purchase and Sale Instructions

Cash and margin accounts

Cash accounts are the most common types of brokerage accounts. They are used by most investors for their simplicity and low risk as an account type. Cash accounts are acceptable accounts for all investor types. Gains in cash accounts are limited by the amount of capital available to the investor. Margin accounts are accounts whereby investors have access to loanable funds, or leverage. The loanable funds are used to magnify gains but have the potential to magnify losses. Investors have the potential to increase the gain in margin accounts by borrowing extra capital to invest and paying it back from the extra gains earned from the extra capital invested. This process works in reverse with losses in margin accounts, increasing the potential for losses. The investor must also pay a rate of interest on the loaned funds in a margin account. Only sophisticated and experienced investors who understand the implications of margin accounts and seek speculative gains should use margin accounts.

Settlement dates

The settlement date in securities trading is the day that the trades actually settle, or securities change hands, as opposed to the execution date, which is the day the trade goes through. If a trade's settlement date is one business day after the execution date, then T + 1 applies; if two days, then T + 2; and if three days, then T + 3.

T + 3 is shorthand for **regular way settlement**. T + 3 is called regular way settlement because most securities trades, but not all, settle this way. Stocks, corporate and municipal bonds, and securities issued by agencies of the federal government all settle regular way.

Important dates

The following dates are in order from first to last to occur:
- Declaration date: This is the date on which the payment of a dividend is announced. Included in the announcement will be the amount of the dividend per share, the ex-dividend date, and the payment date.
- Ex-dividend date: This is the date at which point the seller of the security will be entitled to the dividend payment. Thus, if an investor purchased the security after the ex-dividend date, the seller, not the buyer, would be entitled to the dividend and the security is said to trade ex-dividend.

- Record date: On the record date, the company determines the current equity security holders, as those are the individuals who will receive the dividend. Thus, the ex-dividend date determines that any trades placed after the ex-dividend date would not have settled by the time the dividend payment occurred, thus the seller should still be entitled to the dividend.
- Payment date: The payment date is the date on which dividends are actually distributed to investors.

Rule 10b-10 of the Securities Exchange Act of 1934

Information provided to the customer

Under Rule 10b-10 of the Securities Exchange Act of 1934, a broker or dealer is required, at or before the sale of a security, to disclose the following information:

1. The date and time of the transaction (or that such information will be provided upon completion of the transaction)
2. The identity, price, and number of shares or units of each security sold or purchased
3. The name of the person from whom the security was purchased, or to whom it was sold, or the fact that this information will be provided upon the customer's written request
4. The amount of any remuneration received by the broker from the transaction, unless governed by a previously written agreement with the customer on a basis other than transactional
5. Whether the customer paid any odd-lot fees in connection with the transaction

Disclosure requirements

The disclosure requirements prior to or at the time of a transaction allow customers to monitor all trades being placed on their behalf. This is important not only so that customers can monitor the identify, amount, and price of securities that are bought and sold in their accounts, but also so that they can monitor the efficiency with which any orders are being executed. Additionally, the compensation disclosures provide important information to customers to ensure that their brokers and dealers are not receiving unfair compensation that could either sway the broker or dealers recommendations or reduce the performance of the customer's investments. Finally, several of the disclosure requirements and the statement about availability of additional information help to provide less sophisticated investors with guidance about the critical issues they need to be considering and monitoring. The timeliness in which this information is furnished, which is also governed by Rule 10b-10, is important to allowing the customer to make informed decisions about their account using timely, not stale, information.

Forward pricing and late trading

Since the net asset value (NAV) of open-end mutual fund shares is recalculated at the end of each trading day, and since investors wish to buy or sell mutual fund shares *during* the day, there has to be a sensible way to put a price tag on their transaction. This is done by forward pricing: using the *next available* NAV for each share bought or sold. This ordinarily involves waiting for the NAV to be computed at the end of the trading day.

Late trading involves purchasing mutual fund shares after the market has closed for the day but still obtaining that day's closing price, not the next day's price. This practice is illegal.

Frozen accounts

When an account is frozen, all open orders must be canceled. No further transactions may take place in the account. No money may be withdrawn from or deposited to the account. The assets may not be moved to another account. No action at all may be taken with the account. This usually occurs when an account has been identified as potentially aiding terrorist or drug activity. Freezing may also occur when the owner of the account has died. This is to prevent fraudulent activity from occurring in the owners account. These accounts are especially easy targets, as there is no one to report suspicious activity.

There are different levels of restricted accounts. The most common type of restriction is a trading restriction on the account. In this case, cash may still be withdrawn and usually assets may be transferred, but transactions may not occur in the account. This is usually due to improper documentation on file. Once the documentation is resolved, the restriction is removed.

Obtaining negotiable instruments drawn from a customer's account

Generally speaking, FINRA Rule 4514 prohibits a member or associated person from obtaining checks drafts or other negotiable instruments from customers. However, in the case where the customer has provided express written authorization, this may be permitted. The written authorization may be included on the instrument itself, or may be provided separately. If provided separately, the member or associated person involved in the transaction must maintain a copy of the authorization for at least three years from the date on which the authorization expires. The same record keeping requirements do not apply if the authorization is provided directly on the negotiable instrument. As with the other FINRA rules related to the maintenance of records, this rule is meant to protect customers and ensure that a proper paper trail can be constructed to resolve any potential disputes between members or associated persons and their customers.

Changing an account's name

FINRA rule 4515 sets forth clear guidelines with respect to the approval and documentation required in order to change the name or designation of an account. In order for the change in name or designation to be executed, a qualified registered principal of the member must authorize the change. Additionally, it is incumbent upon that qualified registered principal to be informed of all facts relative to the change and to record his approval either on the order itself or on some other documentation to be included in the file. All of the facts surrounding the change must be documented in writing and maintained in accordance with the rules regarding time and accessibility set forth in SEA Rule 17a-4(b). This protection is important to investors because it ensures that each change has been reviewed by a registered principal, and also because it ensures that a written record of the facts of the case will be maintained.

Timing of a trade execution and account name change

Under FINRA Rule 4515, there are specific guidelines in place relating to the timing of trade execution when changes have been made to the account name or designation. More specifically, Rule 4515 states that all required approval and documentation surrounding the change of an account name or designation must be completed prior to the execution of any trades. Thus, the rule is attempting to eliminate the possible of trades being placed in error or trades being placed in which not all of the required approvals or documentation have been completed, which may result in a trade being placed without the proper authority or under the wrong account name. This safeguarding of customer accounts is an important protection to investors and provides clear guidelines for members and associated persons on the actions required of them when changes are made to an account.

Best execution and interpositioning

Best execution and interpositioning (Rule 5310) - a member must use due diligence in ensuring that the transaction is made on the market best for the security so the price to the customer is favorable. Additionally, a member cannot put a 3rd party between himself and the best market, unless there is an acceptable circumstance. Displaying priced quotations in multiple quotation mediums (Rule 6438) - if a member displays quotes on multiple real-time quotation mediums, the same priced quotes for a security are to be displayed in each medium.
Recording of quotation information (Rule 6430) - any OTC market maker that displays real-time quotes must keep record of certain information including the submitting firm, inter-dealer quotation system, trade date, time quote displayed, security name and symbol, bid and bid quote size, offer and offer quote size, prevailing inside bid, and prevailing inside offer.

COD orders

FINRA Rule 11860 prohibits cash on delivery transactions for securities unless the transaction adheres to a strict set of rules. Before the transaction is entered into, the FINRA member must be aware that the transaction will be cash on delivery, the transaction should be marked as such, and the customer must receive a confirmation of the transaction by the end of the next business day. The FINRA member must receive a signed agreement from the customer stating that the "customer will furnish his agent instructions with respect to the receipt or delivery of the securities involved in the transaction promptly upon receipt by the customer of each confirmation, or the relevant data as to each execution" to help ensure that good and prompt delivery is made.

Customer account statements

NASD Rule 2340 - Customer account statements - members are to send an account statement at least once a quarter to customers that contains a description of any positions, money balances, or account activity, unless there has been none in the quarter. The account statement is to include a statement advising customers to promptly report any inaccuracies in the account statement.
DPP/REIT Securities - a member may provide an estimated per share value to the customer for direct participation programs (DPPs) or real estate investment trusts (REITs).

FINRA Rule 4513

According to FINRA Rule 4513 Records of Written Customer Complaints, a customer complaint refers to any grievance by a customer or any person authorized to act on behalf of the customer involving the activities of the member or a person associated with the member in connection with the solicitation or execution of any transactions or the disposition of securities or funds of that customer. Each member is required to maintain for a period of at least four years copies of all such written customer complaints relating to that office and any actions taken by the member in response, including all related correspondence. Members have the office, instead of keeping records at the office of supervisory jurisdiction, to make records promptly available at FINRA's request in such locations.

FINRA 8000 series

Availability of manual to customers (FINRA Rule 8110) - a member is to make a current copy of the FIRNA Manual available to customers upon their request. Provision of information and testimony and inspection and copying of books (FINRA Rule 8210) - an Adjudicator on FINRA staff has the right to require a member or associated person to provide information and to testify. He also has the right to inspect books and records. FINRA may, under an agreement with another regulatory organization, share information for regulatory purposes.

Code of procedure

Purpose and application- the Code of Procedure outlines the proceedings for disciplining a member or person associated; proceedings for regulating the activities of a member with financial or operational difficulties; proceedings for suspension, cancellation, bars, prohibitions, or limitations; and proceedings for obtaining relief from FINRA eligibility requirements.
Definitions (Rule 9120)
A. Adjudicator - a person or group that presides over a proceeding and renders a decision or recommendation.
B. Chief Hearing Officer - designated by the CEO of FINRA to manage the Office of Hearing Officers.
C. Counsel to the National Adjudicatory Council - an attorney of the Office of the General Counsel of FINRA responsible for advising the National Adjudicatory Council.
D. Extended Hearing Panel - an adjudicator that conducts an extended hearing.
E. Extended Proceeding Committee - an appellate adjudicator that participates in the National Adjudicatory Council's consideration of an extended proceeding.

Code of arbitration procedure

Failure to act under provisions of Code of Arbitration procedure for customer/industry disputes (IM-12000 and IM-13000) - it may be deemed inconsistent with just and equitable principles of trade, and a violation of FINRA rules, to fail to comply with the Code of Arbitration Procedure for Customer/Industry Disputes.
Agreement of the parties (Rules 12105 and 13105) - if the Code allows it, the parties may agree to modify a provision of the Code, but the written agreement of all named parties is required.

Mediation ground rules

Mediation under the Code (Rule 14104) - mediation is voluntary, and requires written agreement from all parties. Any matter that is eligible for arbitration may be mediated, if all parties agree.

Effect of mediation on arbitration proceedings (Rule 14105) - unless the parties agree, a mediation will not delay an arbitration pending FINRA.

Mediation ground rules (Rule 14109) - mediation is voluntary, and a party may withdrawal. The mediator is to be a neutral 3rd party and does not have authority to make decisions. All parties are to initially meet with the mediator to determine to course of the proceedings. The parties agree in good faith to come to a settlement. Mediation is private and confidential.

Practice Test

Practice Questions

1. Which signifies the maximum amount of equity shares a public company can issue?
    a. Issued shares
    b. Total Preferred stock
    c. Authorized shares
    d. Total Common stock

2. What is the record date of a dividend?
    a. The date on which the Board of Directors decides to pay a dividend
    b. The date by which a shareholder must own the stock in order to receive the dividend
    c. The date the dividend will be paid
    d. A date set by FINRA or NYSE

3. How does the Securities Exchange Act of 1934 affect the rights of shareholders?
    a. It requires public companies to report financial information to both the SEC and the general public
    b. It sets penalties for companies that do not meet certain financial expectations
    c. It requires companies to register any offer or sale of securities
    d. It regulates the securities exchanges

4. Which type of Preferred stock can be exchanged for Common by decision of the owner?
    a. Callable Preferred
    b. Participating Preferred
    c. Adjustable Preferred
    d. Convertible Preferred

5. What is the "cooling-off period" for a public offering of securities?
    a. A period of 20 days in which the preliminary prospectus is prepared and reviewed by the SEC
    b. A period of 30 days in which the preliminary prospectus is prepared and reviewed by the SEC
    c. A period of 30 days after filing the preliminary prospectus with the SEC during which no securities may be sold
    d. A period of 20 days after filing the preliminary prospectus with the SEC during which no securities may be sold

6. In which market are the initial offerings of securities sold?
   a. Secondary market
   b. Over the Counter market
   c. Primary market
   d. Auction market

7. How do rising interest rates affect the price of a bond?
   a. There is no change in the price of the bond
   b. The price of the bond decreases
   c. The price of the bond increases
   d. The bond will offer a higher interest rate

8. In a bond investment, which of the following pays periodic interest payments but also repays the principal in one lump sum?
   a. Serial maturity
   b. Balloon Maturity
   c. Variable maturity
   d. Term maturity

9. What is the dollar value of one bond point?
   a. $1
   b. $10
   c. $100
   d. None of the above

10. Which of the following corporations would be regulated under the Trust Indenture Act of 1939?
   a. A corporation that issues $1,000,000 in bonds with a maturity period of one year
   b. A corporation that issues $5,000,000 in bonds with a maturity period of ten years
   c. A corporation that issues $5,000,000 in bonds with a maturity period of one year
   d. A corporation that issues $1,000,000 in bonds with a maturity period of ten years

11. What type of government security has a maturity period of between two and 10 years?
   a. T-notes
   b. T-bills
   c. T-bonds
   d. Treasury receipts

12. What factor determines if a municipal bond will be taxed at the local level?
    a. The bondholder's residence and location where bond was issued
    b. The bondholder's residence only
    c. The amount of interest received by the bondholder
    d. The amount of time the bondholder owned the bond

13. What type of risk refers to an issuer unable to make interest payments on its bond?
    a. Power/constant dollar risk
    b. Junk bond risk
    c. Default/credit risk
    d. Interest rate risk

14. Which issuer's security is backed by the full faith and credit of the US Government?
    a. FNMA
    b. Freddie Mac
    c. GNMA
    d. None of the above

15. What is the name of the rate banks charge other banks for a loan?
    a. Discount rate
    b. Broker call loan rate
    c. Federal funds rate
    d. Prime rate

16. Which is not considered a security?
    a. Certificates of interest
    b. Certificates of interest or participation in profit
    c. Certificates of deposit
    d. Fractional undivided interests in mineral rights

17. What type of securities may be issued under Regulation D?
    a. Limited partnerships
    b. Mutual funds
    c. Restricted securities under Rule 144
    d. Private placements

18. Under which Regulation D rule can companies sell securities totaling less than one million dollars per year?
    a. Rule 504
    b. Rule 505
    c. Rule 506
    d. Rule 507

19. Which condition or event would cause the SEC to revoke a pending registration of a broker-dealer or representative?
    a. Bribing a customer to purchase a security
    b. Business misconduct by an issuer
    c. Failure to meet business objectives
    d. Non-sufficient funds in a personal banking account

20. Which is exempt from registration under FINRA Rule 1032?
    a. A floor member of a national securities exchange
    b. A futures trader registered with a futures association
    c. The assistant to the General Principal
    d. All of the above

21. According to FINRA, what is the definition of a branch office?
    a. Any place where customer orders and reviewed
    b. Any place where orders are executed
    c. Any place where investment banking or securities business is conducted
    d. Any place where private placements are structured

22. What condition must be satisfied before an employee of a FINRA member firm can accept employment or compensation from another business?
    a. The member firm must authorize the employee's employment
    b. None, an employee can work for another business without the member's knowledge
    c. The member firm must be verbally notified
    d. The member firm must be notified in writing

23. What charge may result from a registered representative generating an abnormally large amount of commissions?
    a. Fraud
    b. Churning
    c. Unauthorized trading
    d. Selling away

24. Which amendment to the Securities Exchange Act of 1934 allowed the Securities And Exchange Commission to delegate powers to self-regulatory organizations?
    a. The Uniform Practice Code
    b. The Maloney Act
    c. The code of procedure
    d. None of the above

25. Under what type of retirement plan does an employer contribute a certain amount to an employee's retirement fund each year?
    a. Defined benefit plan
    b. Deferred compensation plan
    c. Payroll deduction plan
    d. Defined contribution plan

26. Which retirement plan can be used by self-employed individuals who want to exempt certain employees from coverage?
    a. Keogh plan
    b. SEP-IRA
    c. Tax sheltered annuity
    d. Roth IRA

27. On which person is the maximum contribution limit based for an Educational Savings Account (ESA)?
    a. The person that pays into the account
    b. The person controlling the account
    c. The parent
    d. The child

28. Which section of the Securities Act of 1933 states that misrepresentations or omissions of material fact are prohibited in the issuer's written and oral communications?
    a. Section 8
    b. Section 11
    c. Section 12
    d. Section 17

29. Under Rule 2210, which does not fall under FINRA's regulation of online mutual fund advertising?
    a. Advertisements intended for small audiences
    b. Correspondence intended for a single customer
    c. Sales literature intended for a targeted audience
    d. Live forum communications

30. FINRA Conduct Rule 2211 exempts which type of institutional sales material and correspondence?
    a. Correspondence sent to more than 25 existing retail customers within 15 calendar days
    b. Correspondence sent to less than 25 existing retail customers within 15 calendar days
    c. Correspondence sent to less than 25 existing retail customers within 30 calendar days
    d. Correspondence sent to more than 25 existing retail customers within 30 calendar days

31. Which situation, according to FINRA, does not constitute a business relationship?
  a. A customer with a current security position with a member broker-dealer
  b. The firm has done business with the person in the past 18 months
  c. A person who inquired about products sold by the firm within the past three months
  d. A person who inquired about products sold by the firm within the past 18 months

32. Which FINRA rule governs how customer complaints are to be handled?
  a. Rule 2211
  b. Rule 3010
  c. Rule 3110
  d. Rule 3040

33. Which type of investor would be best equipped to invest in volatile stocks?
  a. An investor looking for investment growth without taxation
  b. An investor that wants cash flow at periodic intervals
  c. An investor with a high liquid net worth
  d. None of the above

34. Which assessment is most important when determining specific stocks to recommend to a client?
  a. Time horizon
  b. The client's age
  c. The client's current income
  d. Risk tolerance

35. Which type of mutual fund offers shares on a continual basis, issues Common stock and invest in bonds.
  a. Closed-end mutual fund
  b. Open-end mutual fund
  c. Both closed-end and open-end mutual funds
  d. Neither closed-end nor open-end mutual funds

36. What is the public offering price for a mutual fund with a net asset value of $17.50 and a 10% sales charge?
  a. $15.75
  b. $19.44
  c. $17.50
  d. $19.25

37. What method can an investor use to reduce the sales charge on multiple purchases of shares of the same mutual fund?
    a. Use breakpoints
    b. Purchase a closed-end mutual fund
    c. Purchase an open-end mutual fund
    d. Sign a letter of intent

38. A capital gain in a mutual fund is taxed as a short-term gain when...
    a. the investor holds the mutual fund shares for less than one year
    b. the mutual fund holds the underlying security for less than one year
    c. the investor has owned the fund shares for less than one year, and the fund holds the security for less than one year
    d. the fund holds the security for less than one year, and the investor sells his shares

39. According to FINRA rules, when can a mutual fund advertise itself as "diversified?"
    a. When the mutual fund manages more than five different types of funds
    b. When the mutual fund fulfills the 75/5/10 rule
    c. When the mutual fund manages more than 10 different types of funds
    d. When the mutual fund fulfills the 75/10/5 rule

40. Which type of bond fund provides an investor the highest tax advantage?
    a. Corporate bond fund
    b. Government bond fund
    c. Municipal bond fund
    d. Tax-deferred bond fund

41. Which is not part of the criteria in the Investment Company Act of 1940 requirement for an investment fund to be considered a mutual fund?
    a. A minimum of 100 investors
    b. A minimum of $100,000 in seed money
    c. Must have sponsors, a board of directors, investment advisors, transfer agents and custodians
    d. Must maintain a diversified portfolio that follows the 75-5-10 rule

42. What must happen before a mutual fund can assess 12B-1 fees to customers?
    a. The fees must be approved by the SEC
    b. A majority vote from the board of directors
    c. A majority vote from the Board of Directors and the shareholders
    d. Fees must be stated in the fund prospectus

43. Which type of investment sells bonds to investors as equity stakes?
    a. Unit investment trust
    b. Contractual plan
    c. Face amount certificate
    d. Front-end load contractual plan

44. Money market securities must mature in how many months?
    a. 6
    b. 12
    c. 13
    d. 24

45. Which type of settlement option for a variable annuity allows the annuitant to make withdrawals in any amount he chooses?
    a. Unit refund life annuity
    b. Joint and last survivor
    c. Random withdrawal
    d. Life with period certain

46. Which type of insurance plan guarantees a minimum cash value and a certain growth rate?
    a. Variable universal life insurance
    b. Universal life insurance
    c. Temporary insurance
    d. Term life insurance

47. Which federal Act requires that variable life insurance policies and variable annuities must be registered with the SEC before being sold?
    a. Investment Company Act of 1940
    b. Investment Advisors Act of 1940
    c. Securities Exchange Act of 1934
    d. Securities Exchange Act of 1933

48. What type of fee does a mutual fund incur in conjunction with activities reflected in its portfolio turnover rate?
    a. Front-end sales load fee
    b. Commission fee on trading activity
    c. Redemption fee
    d. Deferred sales charge

49. Which is a feature of a UTMA account but not of a UGMA account?
    a. Cannot be a margin account
    b. Re-registration can be extended to age 25
    c. Contributions to the account are irrevocable
    d. Only one adult can manage the account

50. FINRA Rule 3370 allows a member firm and its registered persons to accept purchase orders from customers when...

    a. the customer maintains a margin balance that is sufficient to cover the amount of the purchase order

    b. the securities received against payment are valued at more than the amount of the execution

    c. the customer has been a client of the member firm for more than two years

    d. the securities received against payment are the same amount as the execution

Answers and Explanations

1. C: Authorized shares. The maximum number of shares a corporation may issue, authorized shares is first set in a corporation's Articles of Incorporation. They may be changed only by shareholder vote. Authorized shares govern the distribution of Common stock. Issued shares are Common shares that are actually held collectively by the shareholders, either through purchase directly from the company or on the open market, or through the company's issuance of shares as compensation to insiders. The number of issued shares will be an amount up to the number of authorized shares.

2. B: The date by which an investor must own the stock in order to receive the dividend. On the declaration date, the board declares the dividend and explains who will receive it. Investors are entitled to a dividend if they own the stock on or before a certain date, known as the record date. The board also selects a date upon which the dividend payment will be made, called the payable date. The ex-date (or ex-dividend date) is set by FINRA/NYSE. If a stock is purchased on or after the ex-date, an investor is not entitled to a dividend because he will not become the owner "of record" of the share until after the record date.

3. A: It requires public companies to report financial information to both the SEC and to the general public. The Securities Exchange Act of 1934 requires publicly owned companies to report financial information to the SEC and the general public. Companies must file quarterly (10-Q) and annual reports (10-K) to the SEC, and make these reports available to shareholders and the public. Shareholders also have the right to examine meeting minutes, lists of shareholders and any other company record. The Securities Act of 1933 regulates the offer and sale of securities. It also requires that these securities be registered.

4. D: Convertible Preferred. Convertible Preferred stock can be exchanged for Common stock. One share of Convertible Preferred is generally worth multiple shares of Common stock and the exchange rate is expressed using a ratio. Callable Preferred stock can be repurchased by the issuing corporation at a set date and at a set price. Participating Preferred shares can earn a dividend higher than the rate listed on the stock certificate at the approval of the board of directors. Adjustable Preferred does not have a fixed rate of return; the rate of return changes with an independent economic indicator such as the T-bill rate.

5. D: A period of 20 days after filing the preliminary prospectus with the SEC during which no securities may be sold. The underwriters of an initial public offering (IPO), which may be broker-dealers or investment bankers, complete the paperwork for companies that will be going through the IPO process. They fill out registration statements (or S1s), generate interest for the stock and circulate shares through the primary market. The issuing company and its underwriters go through a mandatory cooling off period after filing the preliminary prospectus with the SEC. This lasts a minimum of 20 days, during which the company cannot sell shares or promote its intended offering within the investment community. It can, however, distribute the preliminary prospectus, commonly called a red herring, to potential investors, with follow-up at the conclusion of the cooling-off period.

6. C: Primary market. IPO stock is sold into the primary market, which is also called the "new issue market." Any trading of the security subsequent to the IPO is done in the secondary market, when an investor sells shares through a brokerage and via a stock exchange to another investor. Exchanges such as the New York Stock Exchange (NYSE) and American Stock Exchange (now called NYSE Amex Equities) are actual, physical locations where stocks are bid, bought and sold by traders. The Over the Counter (OTC) and NASDAQ markets are not physical places but electronic systems over which trades are conducted. In the US, most regional exchanges such as the Pacific, Boston and Philadelphia are still in operation but have been acquired by either the NYSE or NASDAQ. The exchange market is also referred to as the auction market.

7. B: The price of the bond decreases. An existing bond's worth is determined by fluctuations in interest rates: If rates increase, corporations issue new bonds paying a higher nominal yield. If rates decrease, corporations issue new bonds paying a lower nominal yield. Since bonds do not trade at par (face value) in the secondary market, a bond that may have originally sold for $1,500 will not likely sell for $1,500 in the secondary market if interest rates rise. If an existing bond pays 10% and interest rates increase, a corporation will issue new bonds at a higher rate, making the older 10% bonds less attractive investments because investors can purchase new bonds that pay the higher rate. A holder of an existing 10% bond wishing to sell will have to discount the value below par to make it attractive to a potential buyer.

8. D: Term maturity. Bonds are debt securities, or loans, and can be repaid in one of three ways: term maturity, serial maturity or balloon maturity. Term maturity denotes that periodic interest payments are made, with the principal paid in one lump sum on a specific date. A serial maturity bond, often issued by governments as part of a set of bonds, matures at periodic intervals, with both the principal and interest covered. A balloon maturity is a structure that pays off the principal at the end of the loan term, with the final payment substantially larger than the previous payments. Variable maturity describes a particular strategy of buying and selling bonds rather than the structure of an individual bond.

9. B: $10. Bond prices are quoted using bond points, with each point equaling $10. A quote of "85" or "107" would indicate that those bonds are selling at $850 and $1,070, respectively. Simply multiply the point value by 10. Fractional points are also used when quoting bond prices and are expressed as a fraction of 10, therefore ½ equals $5 and ¼ equals $2.50. A bond trading at 105 ⅛ would have a dollar value of $1,051.25 (105 = $1,050 + 1/8 =$1.25).

10. C: A corporation that issues $5,000,000 in bonds with a maturity period of one year. The Trust Indenture Act of 1939 regulates corporations that issue $5,000,000 or more in bonds with maturities of a year or longer. These corporations must sign a contract, also known as an indenture, with a trustee who protects the interest of bondholders. In the event of a default, the indenture trustee can compel the issuer to sell assets through a bankruptcy court and transfer the proceeds to the bondholders as recovery. In some cases, issuers may decide to designate specific assets as collateral against defaulting payments. The titles to those items are then pledged to the trustee, who will begin selling them if the issuer's payments fall behind.

11. A: T-notes. T-notes, short for Treasury Notes, have maturities as short as two years and as long as 10 years, with other maturities of three, five and seven years. T-bonds, or Treasury Bonds, are issued with maturities of between 10 and 30 years, with 30 being the most common. Quotes for both securities are quoted in 1/32s. T-bills, or Treasury Bills, are government securities that repay only the face amount with terms from 4, 13, 26 or 52 weeks. There is no coupon rate and no interest installments associated with T-bills. When investors purchase T-bills, they are seeking the largest discount possible off the face amount. Treasury receipts, which are similar to treasury strips, are purchased at a discount and paid at face value upon maturity. There is no interest payment, but because the par value is increased every year, the investor receives more than he paid.

12. A: The bondholder's residence and location where bond was issued. Two factors determine whether the interest generated by a municipal bond will be taxed at the local level; where the bondholder lives and where the municipal bond was issued. If an investor holds a municipal bond issued by the state of Texas and the bondholder resides in Texas, the state government isn't likely to tax the bond. However, if the bondholder resides in Oklahoma, the state government of Oklahoma could levy a tax. The same principle applies to city issued municipal bonds. If an investor holds a municipal bond issued by the city of Austin, Texas and the bondholder lives in Austin, the bond isn't likely to be taxed by the city. But, if the bondholder moves to Dallas, a tax becomes likely.

13. C: Default/credit risk. Default/credit risk occurs when an issuer is unable to make interest payments on its bonds. Interest rate risk occurs when interest rates rise above an existing bond's fixed coupon rate, thus decreasing a bond's value to investors in the secondary market. Investors may turn to adjustable securities instead. Power/constant dollar risk is the risk of inflation and poses a threat to fixed-rate securities, such as bonds. As inflation increases, the purchasing power of a fixed coupon rate decreases.

14. C: GNMA. GNMA, or Ginnie Mae, is the Government National Mortgage Association, and its mortgage-backed securities, issued as pass-through certificates, are supported by the full faith and credit of the US government. The Federal National Mortgage Association, FNMA or Fannie Mae, also issues pass-through certificate securities, but as a publicly traded company, does not offer the same

guarantee on its securities as GNMA. The Federal Home Loan Mortgage Corporation or Freddie Mac, also issues mortgage-backed securities in the form of pass-through certificates, and is likewise a public company, thereby offering no guarantee on its securities.

15. C: Federal Funds Rate. The Federal Funds Rate is the interest rate banks charge each other when they borrow money. The transaction is actually an overnight transfer of funds from the lending institution's available balance held at the Federal Reserve. The Discount Rate refers to the interest rate banks pay to borrow short-term funds from the Federal Reserve Bank. A Broker call loan rate is the short-term interest rate banks charge to broker-dealers who borrow money, usually for use with margin accounts. The Prime Rate is the interest rate at which a bank's best customers can borrow funds, and is usually the base rate from which banks and other lenders determine what to charge for mortgages and small business loans.

16. C: Certificates of Deposit. Under The Securities Act of 1933, a corporation wishing to sell securities to the general public must register the offering with the SEC. Securities are defined as the following types of paper: stocks; bonds; notes; certificates of interest, ownership or participation in profit; sharing agreements; investment contracts; transferable shares; fractional undivided interests in oil, gas or mineral rights; certificates of deposit for a security; temporary or interim certificates of interest or participation in profit, including receipts, warrants, rights, and guarantees; and evidence of indebtedness. Ambiguous language or misleading terminology must be corrected and attempts to circumvent the Act's requirement will lead to a stop order.

17. D: Private placements. According to Regulation D, issuers can sell securities, either equity or debt, through a non-advertised or non-solicited private placement which limits the issuer to offering restricted securities to accredited or "sophisticated" investors. Most issuers under Reg D are smaller companies, many in startup and development phases, and while they're still required to provide proper paperwork and disclosure documentation, the filing requirements are far less intricate and costly than a registration of public securities.

18. A: Rule 504. Rules 504, 505, and 506 are all exemptions under Regulation D. Rule 504 states that if a company sells no more than $1,000,000 (one million) in securities per year, it can sell restricted securities rather than filing a registration statement with the SEC. Rule 505 offers a similar exemption to companies selling up to $5,000,000 (five million) in securities per year, enabling them to sell restricted securities to accredited investors and up to 35 other non-accredited or non-sophisticated investors. Rule 506 enables a company to raise an unlimited amount of capital through the sale of restricted securities to accredited investors and up to 35 other investors who must be sophisticated. The issuer must make available to non-accredited investors generally the same disclosure documents distributed to accredited investors.

19. A: Bribing a customer to purchase a security. The Securities Act of 1934 empowers the SEC's authority to decide who can become registered within the securities market. Before broker-dealers and representatives can register with an investment firm, or before firms can register with an SRO (self regulatory organization), they must complete Form U-4. The SEC reviews these forms and rejects certain applicants if the applicant has been convicted of a felony in the past 10 years or a misdemeanor involving theft, deceit or embezzlement. Certain types of misdemeanors can cause a pending registration to be revoked:

- With respect to securities trading, bribery, perjury, burglary, taking a false oath, making a false report, or conspiracy to commit any of the listed offenses
- Business misconduct as a broker, dealer, investment adviser, bank, insurance company, fiduciary, transfer agent, or any agent whose role is similar to the ones listed
- Theft, larceny, robbery, extortion, counterfeiting, forgery, fraudulent concealment, misappropriation, and fraudulent conversion of securities or funds

20. D: All of the above. FINRA requires registration for all principals and all representatives of all securities firms doing business in the United States. Principals are the people who manage a member organization's investment banking or securities business, such as partners, officers, directors and managers. Representatives are primarily the sales force, and may also have some supervisory functions. Those exempt from registration include:

1) Clerical employees
2) Those not performing work associated with a member's investment banking or securities business
3) Those only filling a member's immediate need for nominal corporate officers or capital participation
4) Those conducting business on the floor of a national securities or commodities exchange and are already registered with their respective organizations, such as securities and commodities traders

21. C: Any place where investment banking or securities business is conducted. FINRA considers any place where a member conducts investment banking or securities business to be a branch office. The member firm can identify these locations to customers and the public in any way. Branch offices may be considered an office of supervisory jurisdiction (OSJ), or non-OSJ. An OSJ is defined by FINRA as any place where the following is conducted:

- Order execution/market making
- Maintaining possession of customer funds and securities
- Reviewing/endorsing customer orders
- Supervising other branch offices
- Structuring public offerings or private placements
- Authorizing new accounts

22. D: The member firm must be notified in writing. A person cannot simultaneously work for a member firm and another organization unless the member firm receives prompt written notice. After the member firm receives written notice, the employee can accept employment or financial compensation from another business, regardless of its nature. The exception to this rule is when a member firm employee receives payments from passive investments, such as limited partnerships and direct participation plans (DPPs).

23. B: Churning. Churning describes excessive securities trading in a customer account by a broker, without regard to the customer's investment objectives, for the purpose of generating commissions for the benefit of the broker. It's a violation of SEC Rule 15c1-7. For the churning charge to be valid, the broker must have been proven to exercise investment decisions in the customer account. Fraud is the broader term that covers an intentional misleading of clients regarding their investments, primarily by misrepresenting facts or conditions, or by withholding material information. Unauthorized trading occurs when a representative executes an order on behalf of a customer without the customer's consent. The term "selling away" refers to the sale of securities by a registered representative in a private transaction without permission from the member firm.

24. B: The Maloney Act. The Maloney Act was an amendment to the Securities Exchange Act of 1934 that allowed the SEC to delegate power to self-regulatory organizations (SROs). The SEC and FINRA are examples of SROs. The Uniform Practice Code ensures that procedures and regulations remain consistent, or uniform, among all member firms. Regardless of where an account is held, the customer can expect adherence to the same set of practices and policies. The code of procedure refers to the set of rules by which the FINRA investigates a breach of proper conduct.

25. D: Defined contribution plan. The 401(k) is an example of a defined contribution plan, wherein an employer contributes to an employee's retirement fund each year through matching a percentage, sometimes up to 100%, of the funds contributed by the employee. The employee has a degree of control over how his retirement funds are invested. This differs from a defined benefit plan, wherein the company controls the risk management of the retirement portfolio and contributes to an employee's retirement fund based on a formula that considers length of employment and salary, among other things. Defined benefit plans may be "qualified benefit plans" or "non-qualified benefit plans." Deferred compensation and payroll deduction plans are non-qualified retirement accounts in which the employer withholds a portion of the employee's paycheck and secures it until retirement.

26. B: SEP-IRA. A SEP-IRA, or Simplified Employee Pension-IRA, is a non-qualified retirement account into which a business owner makes tax deductible contributions. These contributions, made at the discretion of the employer, vest immediately and the IRA holder (employee) can then direct the investment. Keogh retirement plans are used mainly by self-employed persons or unincorporated

businesses. They're qualified plans with higher contribution limits than a SEP-IRA, based on a percentage of the business' pre-tax income. The contribution made to the proprietor's account must equal the contribution made to the employees' accounts. A TSA, or a tax sheltered annuity, is a qualified retirement plan intended for nonprofit organizations. Roth IRAs are funded by after-tax contributions and can be withdrawn from beginning at age 59½. The withdrawn money is not taxed if done so during retirement.

27. D: The child. Parents can use an Educational Savings Account (ESA) to save money for their children's higher education. An ESA is funded by after-tax contributions, with the maximum contribution limit based on the number of children. The dollar amount is subject to change, per the IRS. Distributions from the account are tax-free unless plan rules have been violated. The Section 529 Plan is a common type of ESA. Under 529 plans, holders may contribute larger after-tax sums than are normally allowed and the distributions will be tax-free at the federal level. State taxes may be levied. ESAs are also called Coverdell Accounts and Education IRAs.

28. C: Section 12. Section 12 regulates the distribution of securities information and states that any misrepresentations or omissions of material fact are strictly prohibited in both the issuer's written and oral communications. Section 12 explains the civil liabilities associated with distributing a misleading prospectus and other fraudulent communications. Section 11 states that if a registration statement leaves out, or misrepresents, a material fact concerning its effective date, the issuer and underwriters may incur civil liabilities. Investors can file a suit if damages result from an omission or misrepresentation. Section 17 forbids an issuer from making misleading or false statements concerning the offer or sale of securities.

29. A: Advertisements intended for small audiences. As technology develops and creates new mediums and opportunities for advertisement, FINRA amended Rule 2210 to include provisions for online advertising and communication. Liability is still assessed by examining the advertisement's intended audience. FINRA created four categories for the placement and regulation of electronic media:
    1) Advertisements intended for large audiences
    2) Correspondence intended for a single customer
    3) Sales literature intended for a targeted audience
    4) Live forum communications

30. C: Correspondence sent to less than 25 existing retail customers within 30 calendar days
Approval from a registered principal is required for correspondence sent to more than 25 existing retail customers within 30 calendar days, and if it advertises a certain good or service, or recommends securities. Member firms create their own rules and regulations regarding the approval and registration of institutional sales materials. These rules depend on the size, structure and business activities of the firm and are documented in writing. Not every institutionalized sales material needs

approval from a registered principal prior to its use. The firm works to uphold compliance by providing training and education to people affiliated with the member firm. FINRA requires evidence that the member is following the guidelines.

31. D: A person who inquired about products sold by the firm in the past 18 months A member firm and a person are deemed to have established a business relationship if:

- The person has had an account, money balance or security position with a firm in the past 18 months
- The firm has served as the broker-dealer on record for the person in the 18 months prior to the call
- The person has inquired about the goods and services provided by the firm in the three months prior to the call

FINRA Rule 2212 also regulates the telemarketing activities of member firms, stating that a telemarketer can call only between the hours of 8 AM and 9 PM. This rule does not apply when the person being solicited has a prior business relationship with the caller, or if the person is a broker-dealer or has given the firm permission.

32. C: Rule 3110. Rule 3110, entitled "Books and Records," states that member firms must create and store records of correspondence, accounts, books and memoranda in accordance with the Securities Exchange Act of 1934. These records include customer complaints. Customer complaints are defined as a written statement expressing a grievance against persons associated with a member firm.

- Rule 2211 covers the approval of institutional sales material and correspondence.
- Rule 3010 governs the supervisory system that each member firm must have in place to ensure that representatives, principles and associates comply with FINRA rules and procedures.
- Rule 3040 prohibits any person who works for a member firm from conducting private securities transactions unless written notice is given to the firm.

33. C: An investor with a high liquid net worth. Liquid net worth is the accumulated value of only those assets that are easily convertible into cash, such as securities and savings accounts. An investor with a high liquid net worth is better equipped to invest in volatile stocks. Investors seeking tax relief want investment growth without taxation until their securities have reached maturity. Municipal bonds, annuities and retirement accounts that produce tax-free interest payments are suited to this type of investor. Current income investors want income payments at periodic intervals, monthly, quarterly, or biannually. Debt securities, money market mutual funds or purchase pass-through certificates are among suitable investments instruments for current income investors.

34. D: Risk tolerance. Considering a client's risk tolerance is crucial to planning his investment strategy. How much risk is the investor willing to take on? Representatives must be candid about a security's potential for growth and failure, as well as the price variation it may undergo. Risk-averse or low-risk tolerant clients should keep investment in equity securities to a minimum, while high-risk clients may be more attracted to speculative stock. Many investors have a specific length of time in which they need their investments to mature or, at the very least, produce a certain income. This is called a time horizon. Common stocks can be suitable for investors with a 20-year time horizon. Short-term investors, who expect a return within a few months, are good candidates for money market securities. Investors who need a substantial return within four or five years may be attracted to income-producing securities that also provide inflationary protection, such as government bonds. A client's age determines the type of investment. Older investors often invest in bonds to provide for income and capital preservation. Younger investors are able to absorb more risk, therefore a loss incurred by investment in equity shares can potentially be recouped due to longer time horizons.

35. B: Open-end mutual fund. Open-end mutual funds, which comprise the majority of mutual funds, have no restrictions on the number of shares they can issue, therefore the net asset value (value of a single share) remains constant and investors receive regularly scheduled distributions of additional shares of the fund's common stock. Open-end mutual funds issue Common stock and invest in a mix of securities that can include bonds. They allow for the purchase and sale of shares whenever an investor is willing. Closed-end funds behave like a company that sells stock, selling a fixed number of shares through an IPO, then trading like a company on a stock exchange.

36. B: $19.44. Net Asset Value, or NAV, measures the worth of each separate mutual fund share. NAV is influenced by the appreciation or depreciation of the securities within the fund's portfolio. Determining the offering price is a two-step process:
- Subtract the sales charge percentage from 100% to find the complement. In this example, the answer is .90 (100% - 10%), expressed as a decimal.
- Divide the net asset value ($17.50) by the compliment (.90). In this example, the answer is $17.50 divided by .90 equals $19.44.

37. D: Sign a letter of intent. An investor can purchase mutual fund shares in installments, and reduce overall sales charges, by signing a letter of intent. This will permit the payment of the sales charge at the breakpoint rather than adjusting the breakpoint incrementally. The investor can purchase additional shares with the savings; however, the fund will withhold those shares until the account becomes fully vested. If the investor fails to make the full contribution per the letter of intent, the mutual fund keeps the extra shares and charges the appropriate breakpoint.

38. B: The mutual fund holds the underlying security for less than one year. When a mutual fund sells the securities in its portfolio at a higher price than the purchase price, a capital gain is realized. Capital gains are distributed to investors on an

annual basis and are taxed according to the length of time the securities have been held in the fund. The length of time an investor has owned the fund is irrelevant. If the fund held the security for less than a year, the IRS taxes capital gains at the investor's regular income rate. If the fund held the security for more than a year, the gain is taxed at the long-term rate.

39. B: When the mutual fund fulfills the 75/5/10 rule. Diversification is the primary benefit of mutual fund investment, and mutual funds may set their own level of diversity. According to FINRA, a mutual fund cannot advertise itself as diversified unless it fulfills the 75/5/10 rule:

- 75% of the fund's portfolio must constitute less than 5% of any one security. If an individual stock in the portfolio appreciates to more than 5% of the required 75%, the fund must refrain from purchasing additional shares of that particular security
- The mutual fund cannot own more than 10% of the outstanding shares of any one company

40. C: Municipal bond fund. Municipal bond funds are a subcategory of bond funds that, along with corporate and government bond funds, focus on the primary objective of income. Municipal bonds are attractive to investors seeking tax incentives in addition to a reliable income stream. An investor interested in generating maximum income may consider corporate bonds, but they're the most susceptible to default risk. A risk-averse investor may turn to government bond funds, which provide capital preservation.

41. D: Must maintain a diversified portfolio that follows the 75/5/10 rule. In addition to FINRA (regulator of the 75/5/10 rule), fund companies must conform to the Investment Company Act of 1940. The Act regulates and classifies investment companies. In addition, the Act specifies the criteria an investment fund must fulfill in order to be considered a mutual fund; at least 100 investors and $100,000 in seed money, and a five-part structure that includes sponsors, a Board of Directors, investment advisors, transfer agents, and custodians.

42. C: Majority vote from the board of directors and the shareholders. A 12B-1 fee can be assessed in a back-end load, a front-end load, a load on both ends and even a no-load fund. Approval and renewal of a 12B-1 fee requires a majority vote from the board and shareholders combined. When a fund performs its own underwriting or sponsoring, it can pay distribution costs by assessing 12B-1 fees to customers. These fees cover expenses such as printing and disseminating sales literature, creating and mailing prospectuses, hiring sales representatives, and performing any other task associated with finding new investors.

43. A: Unit investment trust. Unit investment trusts (UITs) are bond investments sold to investors as equity stakes. Unlike mutual funds, UITs are fixed trusts which hold a portfolio of bonds, but like mutual funds, the equity stakes are redeemable at

the investor's request. A UIT does not actively trade its investments; it adheres to a buy and hold policy. When the bonds in a UIT portfolio mature, they aren't replaced. A contractual plan, also called a periodic payment plan, allows an investor to purchase, in increments, into a plan trust that buys shares of a mutual fund. Face amount certificates are purchased at a specific face value and then redeemed at a later date for a greater value. A front-end load contractual plan can charge fees as high as 50% in the first year, with lower fees during subsequent years, averaging out to 9% by the time the contract expires.

44. C: 13. Money market securities must mature in 13 months or less, and the average maturity within the portfolio cannot exceed 90 days. Money market mutual fund prospectuses contain a warning that the federal government does not guarantee or insure the securities, and a statement declaring money market securities maintain a worth of $1 per share, with no guarantee of this value moving forward. In other words, past performance does not guarantee future results. Money market portfolios contain securities graded within the top two investment ratings by Standard & Poor's and Moody's. At least 95% of these securities have the highest rating.

45. C: Random withdrawal. Under a random withdrawal settlement option, the annuitant makes withdrawals of any amount.
The annuitant decides on the number of withdrawals, and if he dies before receiving all of the payments, they're transferred to a beneficiary. In a joint and last survivor settlement option, the annuity pays monthly installments over the life of the annuitant and another person. Payments continue until both parties die. In a life with period certain settlement option, the annuitant is guaranteed payments for either the majority of his remaining life or a set number of years. If the annuitant dies before the set number of years expires, the remaining payments are made to a beneficiary.

46. B: Universal life. Universal life insurance is a form of permanent insurance. Whole life and universal life guarantee a minimum cash value and a certain growth rate. The policyholder can borrow a maximum of 90% of the cash value, make withdrawals and use the accrued cash value as loan collateral. A variable universal life insurance policy offers a flexible premium and no fixed schedule for paying premiums. It invests the death benefit and cash value into a separate account and may or may not guarantee a minimum death benefit. Temporary insurance policies feature low premiums but cash value does not increase. Beneficiaries are guaranteed a death benefit only if the holder dies during the term of the policy. A Term Life policy, often considered the simplest type of life insurance policy, is a form of temporary insurance that guarantees a death benefit. Term life insurance charges a low monthly premium and does not accrue cash value.

47. D: Securities Exchange Act of 1933. There are four federal Acts governing variable life insurance policies and variable annuities, but it's the Securities Exchange Act of 1933 that requires those policies and annuities to be registered.

- The Investment Company Act of 1940 states that a separate account is its own investment company
- The Investment Advisors Act of 1940 requires registration of money managers and investment advisors
- The Securities Exchange Act of 1933 requires the registration of variable life insurance policies and variable annuities, and that the buyer receives a prospectus before or during the sales presentation.
- The Securities Exchange Act of 1934 requires the seller of variable life insurance or variable annuities to be registered as a broker-dealer.

48. B: Commission fees on trading activities. A fund's portfolio turnover rate measures the frequency of trading in a mutual fund portfolio. A 40% turnover rate means that 40% of the securities in the fund's overall portfolio are traded each year. These trades generate commissions for the broker or institutional trader who transacts the trade, and the fund, like any investor who buys or sells securities, must pay these charges. A front-end sales load fee is a fee a mutual fund investor pays when purchasing shares of the fund. Deferred sales charges are also called "back-end sales load" fees, and would occur when an investor sells shares in the fund. Both front- and back-end load fees are payable to brokers. Some funds are called "no-load" because they charge no sales fees to the fund purchaser. A redemption fee, like a back-end sales load, may be incurred when a shareholder redeems shares, however, redemption fees are charged in order to defray the administrative and paperwork costs associated with the shareholder's redemption, with those fees paid directly to the fund.

49. B: Re-registration can be extended to age 25. Both the Uniform Gifts to Minors Act (UGMA) and the Uniform Transfer to Minor Act (UTMA) regulate custodial accounts for minors. Nearly all US states have adopted UTMA laws, but some states have certain provisions with respect to these types of custodial accounts. A major difference is that re-registration of an UTMA account can be extended to age 25. Nevertheless, common characteristics for both accounts include:

- Opened for the benefit of a minor
- Managed by an adult custodian
- Cannot be a margin account
- Only one adult and one minor can be attached to any one account
- Contributions are irrevocable and indefeasible
- The account will be re-registered in the minor's name once he or she reaches adulthood

50. D: The securities received against payment are the same amount as the execution. FINRA Rule 3370, entitled "Prompt Receipt and Delivery of Securities," outlines the correct procedure for taking orders to purchase securities. The rule

states that a member firm, and its registered representatives, can only accept a customer purchase order once it has determined that the customer or its agent have agreed to receive securities against payment in the amount equal to the execution. This rule is also useful in regulating an orderly market with respect to shorting, since the registered representative must determine, prior to accepting a short order, that the security will be delivered or borrowed before the settlement date.

Secret Key #1 - Time is Your Greatest Enemy

Pace Yourself

Wear a watch. At the beginning of the test, check the time (or start a chronometer on your watch to count the minutes), and check the time after every few questions to make sure you are "on schedule."

If you are forced to speed up, do it efficiently. Usually one or more answer choices can be eliminated without too much difficulty. Above all, don't panic. Don't speed up and just begin guessing at random choices. By pacing yourself, and continually monitoring your progress against your watch, you will always know exactly how far ahead or behind you are with your available time. If you find that you are one minute behind on the test, don't skip one question without spending any time on it, just to catch back up. Take 15 fewer seconds on the next four questions, and after four questions you'll have caught back up. Once you catch back up, you can continue working each problem at your normal pace.

Furthermore, don't dwell on the problems that you were rushed on. If a problem was taking up too much time and you made a hurried guess, it must be difficult. The difficult questions are the ones you are most likely to miss anyway, so it isn't a big loss. It is better to end with more time than you need than to run out of time.

Lastly, sometimes it is beneficial to slow down if you are constantly getting ahead of time. You are always more likely to catch a careless mistake by working more slowly than quickly, and among very high-scoring test takers (those who are likely to have lots of time left over), careless errors affect the score more than mastery of material.

Secret Key #2 - Guessing is not Guesswork

You probably know that guessing is a good idea. Unlike other standardized tests, there is no penalty for getting a wrong answer. Even if you have no idea about a question, you still have a 20-25% chance of getting it right.

Most test takers do not understand the impact that proper guessing can have on their score. Unless you score extremely high, guessing will significantly contribute to your final score.

Monkeys Take the Test

What most test takers don't realize is that to insure that 20-25% chance, you have to guess randomly. If you put 20 monkeys in a room to take this test, assuming they answered once per question and behaved themselves, on average they would get 20-25% of the questions correct. Put 20 test takers in the room, and the average will be much lower among guessed questions. Why?

1. The test writers intentionally write deceptive answer choices that "look" right. A test taker has no idea about a question, so he picks the "best looking" answer, which is often wrong. The monkey has no idea what looks good and what doesn't, so it will consistently be right about 20-25% of the time.
2. Test takers will eliminate answer choices from the guessing pool based on a hunch or intuition. Simple but correct answers often get excluded, leaving a 0% chance of being correct. The monkey has no clue, and often gets lucky with the best choice.

This is why the process of elimination endorsed by most test courses is flawed and detrimental to your performance. Test takers don't guess; they make an ignorant stab in the dark that is usually worse than random.

$5 Challenge

Let me introduce one of the most valuable ideas of this course—the $5 challenge:

You only mark your "best guess" if you are willing to bet $5 on it.
You only eliminate choices from guessing if you are willing to bet $5 on it.

Why $5? Five dollars is an amount of money that is small yet not insignificant, and can really add up fast (20 questions could cost you $100). Likewise, each answer choice on one question of the test will have a small impact on your overall score, but it can really add up to a lot of points in the end.

The process of elimination IS valuable. The following shows your chance of guessing it right:

If you eliminate wrong answer choices until only this many remain:	Chance of getting it correct:
1	100%
2	50%
3	33%

However, if you accidentally eliminate the right answer or go on a hunch for an incorrect answer, your chances drop dramatically—to 0%. By guessing among all the answer choices, you are GUARANTEED to have a shot at the right answer.

That's why the $5 test is so valuable. If you give up the advantage and safety of a pure guess, it had better be worth the risk.

What we still haven't covered is how to be sure that whatever guess you make is truly random. Here's the easiest way:

Always pick the first answer choice among those remaining.

Such a technique means that you have decided, **before you see a single test question**, exactly how you are going to guess, and since the order of choices tells you nothing about which one is correct, this guessing technique is perfectly random.

This section is not meant to scare you away from making educated guesses or eliminating choices; you just need to define when a choice is worth eliminating. The $5 test, along with a pre-defined random guessing strategy, is the best way to make sure you reap all of the benefits of guessing.

Secret Key #3 - Practice Smarter, Not Harder

Many test takers delay the test preparation process because they dread the awful amounts of practice time they think necessary to succeed on the test. We have refined an effective method that will take you only a fraction of the time.

There are a number of "obstacles" in the path to success. Among these are answering questions, finishing in time, and mastering test-taking strategies. All must be executed on the day of the test at peak performance, or your score will suffer. The test is a mental marathon that has a large impact on your future.

Just like a marathon runner, it is important to work your way up to the full challenge. So first you just worry about questions, and then time, and finally strategy:

Success Strategy

1. Find a good source for practice tests.
2. If you are willing to make a larger time investment, consider using more than one study guide. Often the different approaches of multiple authors will help you "get" difficult concepts.
3. Take a practice test with no time constraints, with all study helps, "open book." Take your time with questions and focus on applying strategies.
4. Take a practice test with time constraints, with all guides, "open book."
5. Take a final practice test without open material and with time limits.

If you have time to take more practice tests, just repeat step 5. By gradually exposing yourself to the full rigors of the test environment, you will condition your mind to the stress of test day and maximize your success.

Secret Key #4 - Prepare, Don't Procrastinate

Let me state an obvious fact: if you take the test three times, you will probably get three different scores. This is due to the way you feel on test day, the level of preparedness you have, and the version of the test you see. Despite the test writers' claims to the contrary, some versions of the test WILL be easier for you than others.

Since your future depends so much on your score, you should maximize your chances of success. In order to maximize the likelihood of success, you've got to prepare in advance. This means taking practice tests and spending time learning the information and test taking strategies you will need to succeed.

Never go take the actual test as a "practice" test, expecting that you can just take it again if you need to. Take all the practice tests you can on your own, but when you go to take the official test, be prepared, be focused, and do your best the first time!

Secret Key #5 - Test Yourself

Everyone knows that time is money. There is no need to spend too much of your time or too little of your time preparing for the test. You should only spend as much of your precious time preparing as is necessary for you to get the score you need.

Once you have taken a practice test under real conditions of time constraints, then you will know if you are ready for the test or not.

If you have scored extremely high the first time that you take the practice test, then there is not much point in spending countless hours studying. You are already there.

Benchmark your abilities by retaking practice tests and seeing how much you have improved. Once you consistently score high enough to guarantee success, then you are ready.

If you have scored well below where you need, then knuckle down and begin studying in earnest. Check your improvement regularly through the use of practice tests under real conditions. Above all, don't worry, panic, or give up. The key is perseverance!

Then, when you go to take the test, remain confident and remember how well you did on the practice tests. If you can score high enough on a practice test, then you can do the same on the real thing.

General Strategies

The most important thing you can do is to ignore your fears and jump into the test immediately. Do not be overwhelmed by any strange-sounding terms. You have to jump into the test like jumping into a pool—all at once is the easiest way.

Make Predictions

As you read and understand the question, try to guess what the answer will be. Remember that several of the answer choices are wrong, and once you begin reading them, your mind will immediately become cluttered with answer choices designed to throw you off. Your mind is typically the most focused immediately after you have read the question and digested its contents. If you can, try to predict what the correct answer will be. You may be surprised at what you can predict.

Quickly scan the choices and see if your prediction is in the listed answer choices. If it is, then you can be quite confident that you have the right answer. It still won't hurt to check the other answer choices, but most of the time, you've got it!

Answer the Question

It may seem obvious to only pick answer choices that answer the question, but the test writers can create some excellent answer choices that are wrong. Don't pick an answer just because it sounds right, or you believe it to be true. It MUST answer the question. Once you've made your selection, always go back and check it against the question and make sure that you didn't misread the question and that the answer choice does answer the question posed.

Benchmark

After you read the first answer choice, decide if you think it sounds correct or not. If it doesn't, move on to the next answer choice. If it does, mentally mark that answer choice. This doesn't mean that you've definitely selected it as your answer choice, it just means that it's the best you've seen thus far. Go ahead and read the next choice. If the next choice is worse than the one you've already selected, keep going to the next answer choice. If the next choice is better than the choice you've already selected, mentally mark the new answer choice as your best guess.

The first answer choice that you select becomes your standard. Every other answer choice must be benchmarked against that standard. That choice is correct until proven otherwise by another answer choice beating it out. Once you've decided that no other answer choice seems as good, do one final check to ensure that your answer choice answers the question posed.

Valid Information

Don't discount any of the information provided in the question. Every piece of information may be necessary to determine the correct answer. None of the information in the question is there to throw you off (while the answer choices will certainly have information to throw you off). If two seemingly unrelated topics are discussed, don't ignore either. You can be confident there is a relationship, or it wouldn't be included in the question, and you are probably going to have to determine what is that relationship to find the answer.

Avoid "Fact Traps"

Don't get distracted by a choice that is factually true. Your search is for the answer that answers the question. Stay focused and don't fall for an answer that is true but irrelevant. Always go back to the question and make sure you're choosing an answer that actually answers the question and is not just a true statement. An answer can be factually correct, but it MUST answer the question asked. Additionally, two answers can both be seemingly correct, so be sure to read all of the answer choices, and make sure that you get the one that BEST answers the question.

Milk the Question

Some of the questions may throw you completely off. They might deal with a subject you have not been exposed to, or one that you haven't reviewed in years. While your lack of knowledge about the subject will be a hindrance, the question itself can give you many clues that will help you find the correct answer. Read the question carefully and look for clues. Watch particularly for adjectives and nouns describing difficult terms or words that you don't recognize. Regardless of whether you completely understand a word or not, replacing it with a synonym, either provided or one you more familiar with, may help you to understand what the questions are asking. Rather than wracking your mind about specific detailed information concerning a difficult term or word, try to use mental substitutes that are easier to understand.

The Trap of Familiarity

Don't just choose a word because you recognize it. On difficult questions, you may not recognize a number of words in the answer choices. The test writers don't put "make-believe" words on the test, so don't think that just because you only recognize all the words in one answer choice that that answer choice must be correct. If you only recognize words in one answer choice, then focus on that one. Is it correct? Try your best to determine if it is correct. If it is, that's great. If not, eliminate it. Each word and answer choice you eliminate increases your chances of getting the question correct, even if you then have to guess among the unfamiliar choices.

Eliminate Answers

Eliminate choices as soon as you realize they are wrong. But be careful! Make sure you consider all of the possible answer choices. Just because one appears right, doesn't mean that the next one won't be even better! The test writers will usually put more than one good answer choice for every question, so read all of them. Don't worry if you are stuck between two that seem right. By getting down to just two remaining possible choices, your odds are now 50/50. Rather than wasting too much time, play the odds. You are guessing, but guessing wisely because you've been able to knock out some of the answer choices that you know are wrong. If you are eliminating choices and realize that the last answer choice you are left with is also obviously wrong, don't panic. Start over and consider each choice again. There may easily be something that you missed the first time and will realize on the second pass.

Tough Questions

If you are stumped on a problem or it appears too hard or too difficult, don't waste time. Move on! Remember though, if you can quickly check for obviously incorrect answer choices, your chances of guessing correctly are greatly improved. Before you completely give up, at least try to knock out a couple of possible answers. Eliminate what you can and then guess at the remaining answer choices before moving on.

Brainstorm

If you get stuck on a difficult question, spend a few seconds quickly brainstorming. Run through the complete list of possible answer choices. Look at each choice and ask yourself, "Could this answer the question satisfactorily?" Go through each answer choice and consider it independently of the others. By systematically going through all possibilities, you may find something that you would otherwise overlook. Remember though that when you get stuck, it's important to try to keep moving.

Read Carefully

Understand the problem. Read the question and answer choices carefully. Don't miss the question because you misread the terms. You have plenty of time to read each question thoroughly and make sure you understand what is being asked. Yet a happy medium must be attained, so don't waste too much time. You must read carefully, but efficiently.

Face Value

When in doubt, use common sense. Always accept the situation in the problem at face value. Don't read too much into it. These problems will not require you to make huge leaps of logic. The test writers aren't trying to throw you off with a cheap trick. If you have to go beyond creativity and make a leap of logic in order to have an answer choice answer the question, then you should look at the other answer choices. Don't overcomplicate the problem by creating theoretical relationships or explanations that will warp time or space. These are normal problems rooted in reality. It's just that the applicable relationship or explanation may not be readily apparent and you have to figure things out. Use your common sense to interpret anything that isn't clear.

Prefixes

If you're having trouble with a word in the question or answer choices, try dissecting it. Take advantage of every clue that the word might include. Prefixes and suffixes can be a huge help. Usually they allow you to determine a basic meaning. Pre- means before, post- means after, pro - is positive, de- is negative. From these prefixes and suffixes, you can get an idea of the general meaning of the word and try to put it into context. Beware though of any traps. Just because con- is the opposite of pro-, doesn't necessarily mean congress is the opposite of progress!

Hedge Phrases

Watch out for critical hedge phrases, led off with words such as "likely," "may," "can," "sometimes," "often," "almost," "mostly," "usually," "generally," "rarely," and "sometimes." Question writers insert these hedge phrases to cover every possibility. Often an answer choice will be wrong simply because it leaves no room for exception. Unless the situation calls for them, avoid answer choices that have definitive words like "exactly," and "always."

Switchback Words

Stay alert for "switchbacks." These are the words and phrases frequently used to alert you to shifts in thought. The most common switchback word is "but." Others include "although," "however," "nevertheless," "on the other hand," "even though," "while," "in spite of," "despite," and "regardless of."

New Information

Correct answer choices will rarely have completely new information included. Answer choices typically are straightforward reflections of the material asked about and will directly relate to the question. If a new piece of information is included in an answer choice that doesn't even seem to relate to the topic being asked about, then that answer choice is likely incorrect. All of the information needed to answer the question is usually provided for you in the question. You should not have to make guesses that are unsupported or choose answer choices that require unknown information that cannot be reasoned from what is given.

Time Management

On technical questions, don't get lost on the technical terms. Don't spend too much time on any one question. If you don't know what a term means, then odds are you aren't going to get much further since you don't have a dictionary. You should be able to immediately recognize whether or not you know a term. If you don't, work with the other clues that you have—the other answer choices and terms provided—but don't waste too much time trying to figure out a difficult term that you don't know.

Contextual Clues

Look for contextual clues. An answer can be right but not the correct answer. The contextual clues will help you find the answer that is most right and is correct. Understand the context in which a phrase or statement is made. This will help you make important distinctions.

Don't Panic

Panicking will not answer any questions for you; therefore, it isn't helpful. When you first see the question, if your mind goes blank, take a deep breath. Force yourself to mechanically go through the steps of solving the problem using the strategies you've learned.

Pace Yourself

Don't get clock fever. It's easy to be overwhelmed when you're looking at a page full of questions, your mind is full of random thoughts and feeling confused, and the clock is ticking down faster than you would like. Calm down and maintain the pace that you have set for yourself. As long as you are on track by monitoring your pace, you are guaranteed to have enough time for yourself. When you get to the last few minutes of the test, it may seem like you won't have enough time left, but if you only have as many questions as you should have left at that point, then you're right on track!

Answer Selection

The best way to pick an answer choice is to eliminate all of those that are wrong, until only one is left and confirm that is the correct answer. Sometimes though, an answer choice may immediately look right. Be careful! Take a second to make sure that the other choices are not equally obvious. Don't make a hasty mistake. There are only two times that you should stop before checking other answers. First is when you are positive that the answer choice you have selected is correct. Second is when time is almost out and you have to make a quick guess!

Check Your Work

Since you will probably not know every term listed and the answer to every question, it is important that you get credit for the ones that you do know. Don't miss any questions through careless mistakes. If at all possible, try to take a second to look back over your answer selection and make sure you've selected the correct answer choice and haven't made a costly careless mistake (such as marking an answer choice that you didn't mean to mark). The time it takes for this quick double check should more than pay for itself in caught mistakes.

Beware of Directly Quoted Answers

Sometimes an answer choice will repeat word for word a portion of the question or reference section. However, beware of such exact duplication. It may be a trap! More than likely, the correct choice will paraphrase or summarize a point, rather than being exactly the same wording.

Slang

Scientific sounding answers are better than slang ones. An answer choice that begins "To compare the outcomes..." is much more likely to be correct than one that begins "Because some people insisted..."

Extreme Statements

Avoid wild answers that throw out highly controversial ideas that are proclaimed as established fact. An answer choice that states the "process should used in certain situations, if…" is much more likely to be correct than one that states the "process should be discontinued completely." The first is a calm rational statement and doesn't even make a definitive, uncompromising stance, using a hedge word "if" to provide wiggle room, whereas the second choice is a radical idea and far more extreme.

Answer Choice Families

When you have two or more answer choices that are direct opposites or parallels, one of them is usually the correct answer. For instance, if one answer choice states "x increases" and another answer choice states "x decreases" or "y increases," then those two or three answer choices are very similar in construction and fall into the same family of answer choices. A family of answer choices consists of two or three answer choices, very similar in construction, but often with directly opposite meanings. Usually the correct answer choice will be in that family of answer choices. The "odd man out" or answer choice that doesn't seem to fit the parallel construction of the other answer choices is more likely to be incorrect.

Special Report: How to Overcome Test Anxiety

The very nature of tests caters to some level of anxiety, nervousness, or tension, just as we feel for any important event that occurs in our lives. A little bit of anxiety or nervousness can be a good thing. It helps us with motivation, and makes achievement just that much sweeter. However, too much anxiety can be a problem, especially if it hinders our ability to function and perform.

"Test anxiety," is the term that refers to the emotional reactions that some test-takers experience when faced with a test or exam. Having a fear of testing and exams is based upon a rational fear, since the test-taker's performance can shape the course of an academic career. Nevertheless, experiencing excessive fear of examinations will only interfere with the test-taker's ability to perform and chance to be successful.

There are a large variety of causes that can contribute to the development and sensation of test anxiety. These include, but are not limited to, lack of preparation and worrying about issues surrounding the test.

Lack of Preparation

Lack of preparation can be identified by the following behaviors or situations:

Not scheduling enough time to study, and therefore cramming the night before the test or exam
Managing time poorly, to create the sensation that there is not enough time to do everything
Failing to organize the text information in advance, so that the study material consists of the entire text and not simply the pertinent information
Poor overall studying habits

Worrying, on the other hand, can be related to both the test taker, or many other factors around him/her that will be affected by the results of the test. These include worrying about:

Previous performances on similar exams, or exams in general
How friends and other students are achieving
The negative consequences that will result from a poor grade or failure

There are three primary elements to test anxiety. Physical components, which involve the same typical bodily reactions as those to acute anxiety (to be discussed below). Emotional factors have to do with fear or panic. Mental or cognitive issues concerning attention spans and memory abilities.

Physical Signals

There are many different symptoms of test anxiety, and these are not limited to mental and emotional strain. Frequently there are a range of physical signals that will let a test taker know that he/she is suffering from test anxiety. These bodily changes can include the following:

Perspiring
Sweaty palms
Wet, trembling hands
Nausea
Dry mouth
A knot in the stomach
Headache
Faintness
Muscle tension
Aching shoulders, back and neck
Rapid heart beat
Feeling too hot/cold

To recognize the sensation of test anxiety, a test-taker should monitor him/herself for the following sensations:

The physical distress symptoms as listed above
Emotional sensitivity, expressing emotional feelings such as the need to cry or laugh too much, or a sensation of anger or helplessness
A decreased ability to think, causing the test-taker to blank out or have racing thoughts that are hard to organize or control.

Though most students will feel some level of anxiety when faced with a test or exam, the majority can cope with that anxiety and maintain it at a manageable level. However, those who cannot are faced with a very real and very serious condition, which can and should be controlled for the immeasurable benefit of this sufferer.

Naturally, these sensations lead to negative results for the testing experience. The most common effects of test anxiety have to do with nervousness and mental blocking.

Nervousness

Nervousness can appear in several different levels:

The test-taker's difficulty, or even inability to read and understand the questions on the test

The difficulty or inability to organize thoughts to a coherent form
The difficulty or inability to recall key words and concepts relating to the testing questions (especially essays)
The receipt of poor grades on a test, though the test material was well known by the test taker

Conversely, a person may also experience mental blocking, which involves:

Blanking out on test questions
Only remembering the correct answers to the questions when the test has already finished.

Fortunately for test anxiety sufferers, beating these feelings, to a large degree, has to do with proper preparation. When a test taker has a feeling of preparedness, then anxiety will be dramatically lessened.

The first step to resolving anxiety issues is to distinguish which of the two types of anxiety are being suffered. If the anxiety is a direct result of a lack of preparation, this should be considered a normal reaction, and the anxiety level (as opposed to the test results) shouldn't be anything to worry about. However, if, when adequately prepared, the test-taker still panics, blanks out, or seems to overreact, this is not a fully rational reaction. While this can be considered normal too, there are many ways to combat and overcome these effects.

Remember that anxiety cannot be entirely eliminated, however, there are ways to minimize it, to make the anxiety easier to manage. Preparation is one of the best ways to minimize test anxiety. Therefore the following techniques are wise in order to best fight off any anxiety that may want to build.

To begin with, try to avoid cramming before a test, whenever it is possible. By trying to memorize an entire term's worth of information in one day, you'll be shocking your system, and not giving yourself a very good chance to absorb the information. This is an easy path to anxiety, so for those who suffer from test anxiety, cramming should not even be considered an option.

Instead of cramming, work throughout the semester to combine all of the material which is presented throughout the semester, and work on it gradually as the course goes by, making sure to master the main concepts first, leaving minor details for a week or so before the test.

To study for the upcoming exam, be sure to pose questions that may be on the examination, to gauge the ability to answer them by integrating the ideas from your texts, notes and lectures, as well as any supplementary readings.

If it is truly impossible to cover all of the information that was covered in that particular term, concentrate on the most important portions, that can be covered very well. Learn these concepts as best as possible, so that when the test comes, a goal can be made to use these concepts as presentations of your knowledge.

In addition to study habits, changes in attitude are critical to beating a struggle with test anxiety. In fact, an improvement of the perspective over the entire test-taking experience can actually help a test taker to enjoy studying and therefore improve the overall experience. Be certain not to overemphasize the significance of the grade - know that the result of the test is neither a reflection of self worth, nor is it a measure of intelligence; one grade will not predict a person's future success.

To improve an overall testing outlook, the following steps should be tried:

Keeping in mind that the most reasonable expectation for taking a test is to expect to try to demonstrate as much of what you know as you possibly can. Reminding ourselves that a test is only one test; this is not the only one, and there will be others.
The thought of thinking of oneself in an irrational, all-or-nothing term should be avoided at all costs.
A reward should be designated for after the test, so there's something to look forward to. Whether it be going to a movie, going out to eat, or simply visiting friends, schedule it in advance, and do it no matter what result is expected on the exam.

Test-takers should also keep in mind that the basics are some of the most important things, even beyond anti-anxiety techniques and studying. Never neglect the basic social, emotional and biological needs, in order to try to absorb information. In order to best achieve, these three factors must be held as just as important as the studying itself.

Study Steps

Remember the following important steps for studying:

Maintain healthy nutrition and exercise habits. Continue both your recreational activities and social pass times. These both contribute to your physical and emotional well being.
Be certain to get a good amount of sleep, especially the night before the test, because when you're overtired you are not able to perform to the best of your best ability.
Keep the studying pace to a moderate level by taking breaks when they are needed, and varying the work whenever possible, to keep the mind fresh instead of getting bored.
When enough studying has been done that all the material that can be learned has been learned, and the test taker is prepared for the test, stop studying and do

something relaxing such as listening to music, watching a movie, or taking a warm bubble bath.

There are also many other techniques to minimize the uneasiness or apprehension that is experienced along with test anxiety before, during, or even after the examination. In fact, there are a great deal of things that can be done to stop anxiety from interfering with lifestyle and performance. Again, remember that anxiety will not be eliminated entirely, and it shouldn't be. Otherwise that "up" feeling for exams would not exist, and most of us depend on that sensation to perform better than usual. However, this anxiety has to be at a level that is manageable.

Of course, as we have just discussed, being prepared for the exam is half the battle right away. Attending all classes, finding out what knowledge will be expected on the exam, and knowing the exam schedules are easy steps to lowering anxiety. Keeping up with work will remove the need to cram, and efficient study habits will eliminate wasted time. Studying should be done in an ideal location for concentration, so that it is simple to become interested in the material and give it complete attention. A method such as SQ3R (Survey, Question, Read, Recite, Review) is a wonderful key to follow to make sure that the study habits are as effective as possible, especially in the case of learning from a textbook. Flashcards are great techniques for memorization. Learning to take good notes will mean that notes will be full of useful information, so that less sifting will need to be done to seek out what is pertinent for studying. Reviewing notes after class and then again on occasion will keep the information fresh in the mind. From notes that have been taken summary sheets and outlines can be made for simpler reviewing.

A study group can also be a very motivational and helpful place to study, as there will be a sharing of ideas, all of the minds can work together, to make sure that everyone understands, and the studying will be made more interesting because it will be a social occasion.

Basically, though, as long as the test-taker remains organized and self confident, with efficient study habits, less time will need to be spent studying, and higher grades will be achieved.

To become self confident, there are many useful steps. The first of these is "self talk." It has been shown through extensive research, that self-talk for students who suffer from test anxiety, should be well monitored, in order to make sure that it contributes to self confidence as opposed to sinking the student. Frequently the self talk of test-anxious students is negative or self-defeating, thinking that everyone else is smarter and faster, that they always mess up, and that if they don't do well, they'll fail the entire course. It is important to decreasing anxiety that awareness is made of self talk. Try writing any negative self thoughts and then disputing them with a positive statement instead. Begin self-encouragement as though it was a friend speaking. Repeat positive statements to help reprogram the mind to believing in successes instead of failures.

Helpful Techniques

Other extremely helpful techniques include:

Self-visualization of doing well and reaching goals
While aiming for an "A" level of understanding, don't try to "overprotect" by setting your expectations lower. This will only convince the mind to stop studying in order to meet the lower expectations.
Don't make comparisons with the results or habits of other students. These are individual factors, and different things work for different people, causing different results.
Strive to become an expert in learning what works well, and what can be done in order to improve. Consider collecting this data in a journal.
Create rewards for after studying instead of doing things before studying that will only turn into avoidance behaviors.
Make a practice of relaxing - by using methods such as progressive relaxation, self-hypnosis, guided imagery, etc - in order to make relaxation an automatic sensation.
Work on creating a state of relaxed concentration so that concentrating will take on the focus of the mind, so that none will be wasted on worrying.
Take good care of the physical self by eating well and getting enough sleep.
Plan in time for exercise and stick to this plan.

Beyond these techniques, there are other methods to be used before, during and after the test that will help the test-taker perform well in addition to overcoming anxiety.

Before the exam comes the academic preparation. This involves establishing a study schedule and beginning at least one week before the actual date of the test. By doing this, the anxiety of not having enough time to study for the test will be automatically eliminated. Moreover, this will make the studying a much more effective experience, ensuring that the learning will be an easier process. This relieves much undue pressure on the test-taker.

Summary sheets, note cards, and flash cards with the main concepts and examples of these main concepts should be prepared in advance of the actual studying time. A topic should never be eliminated from this process. By omitting a topic because it isn't expected to be on the test is only setting up the test-taker for anxiety should it actually appear on the exam. Utilize the course syllabus for laying out the topics that should be studied. Carefully go over the notes that were made in class, paying special attention to any of the issues that the professor took special care to emphasize while lecturing in class. In the textbooks, use the chapter review, or if possible, the chapter tests, to begin your review.

It may even be possible to ask the instructor what information will be covered on the exam, or what the format of the exam will be (for example, multiple choice, essay, free form, true-false). Additionally, see if it is possible to find out how many questions will be on the test. If a review sheet or sample test has been offered by the professor, make good use of it, above anything else, for the preparation for the test. Another great resource for getting to know the examination is reviewing tests from previous semesters. Use these tests to review, and aim to achieve a 100% score on each of the possible topics. With a few exceptions, the goal that you set for yourself is the highest one that you will reach.

Take all of the questions that were assigned as homework, and rework them to any other possible course material. The more problems reworked, the more skill and confidence will form as a result. When forming the solution to a problem, write out each of the steps. Don't simply do head work. By doing as many steps on paper as possible, much clarification and therefore confidence will be formed. Do this with as many homework problems as possible, before checking the answers. By checking the answer after each problem, a reinforcement will exist, that will not be on the exam. Study situations should be as exam-like as possible, to prime the test-taker's system for the experience. By waiting to check the answers at the end, a psychological advantage will be formed, to decrease the stress factor.

Another fantastic reason for not cramming is the avoidance of confusion in concepts, especially when it comes to mathematics. 8-10 hours of study will become one hundred percent more effective if it is spread out over a week or at least several days, instead of doing it all in one sitting. Recognize that the human brain requires time in order to assimilate new material, so frequent breaks and a span of study time over several days will be much more beneficial.

Additionally, don't study right up until the point of the exam. Studying should stop a minimum of one hour before the exam begins. This allows the brain to rest and put things in their proper order. This will also provide the time to become as relaxed as possible when going into the examination room. The test-taker will also have time to eat well and eat sensibly. Know that the brain needs food as much as the rest of the body. With enough food and enough sleep, as well as a relaxed attitude, the body and the mind are primed for success.

Avoid any anxious classmates who are talking about the exam. These students only spread anxiety, and are not worth sharing the anxious sentimentalities.

Before the test also involves creating a positive attitude, so mental preparation should also be a point of concentration. There are many keys to creating a positive attitude. Should fears become rushing in, make a visualization of taking the exam, doing well, and seeing an A written on the paper. Write out a list of affirmations that will bring a feeling of confidence, such as "I am doing well in my English class," "I studied well and know my material," "I enjoy this class." Even if the affirmations aren't believed at first, it sends a positive message to the subconscious which will result in an alteration of the overall belief system, which is the system that creates reality.

If a sensation of panic begins, work with the fear and imagine the very worst! Work through the entire scenario of not passing the test, failing the entire course, and dropping out of school, followed by not getting a job, and pushing a shopping cart through the dark alley where you'll live. This will place things into perspective! Then, practice deep breathing and create a visualization of the opposite situation - achieving an "A" on the exam, passing the entire course, receiving the degree at a graduation ceremony.

On the day of the test, there are many things to be done to ensure the best results, as well as the most calm outlook. The following stages are suggested in order to maximize test-taking potential:

Begin the examination day with a moderate breakfast, and avoid any coffee or beverages with caffeine if the test taker is prone to jitters. Even people who are used to managing caffeine can feel jittery or light-headed when it is taken on a test day.

Attempt to do something that is relaxing before the examination begins. As last minute cramming clouds the mastering of overall concepts, it is better to use this time to create a calming outlook.

Be certain to arrive at the test location well in advance, in order to provide time to select a location that is away from doors, windows and other distractions, as well as giving enough time to relax before the test begins.

Keep away from anxiety generating classmates who will upset the sensation of stability and relaxation that is being attempted before the exam.

Should the waiting period before the exam begins cause anxiety, create a self-distraction by reading a light magazine or something else that is relaxing and simple.

During the exam itself, read the entire exam from beginning to end, and find out how much time should be allotted to each individual problem. Once writing the exam, should more time be taken for a problem, it should be abandoned, in order to begin another problem. If there is time at the end, the unfinished problem can always be returned to and completed.

Read the instructions very carefully - twice - so that unpleasant surprises won't follow during or after the exam has ended.

When writing the exam, pretend that the situation is actually simply the completion of homework within a library, or at home. This will assist in forming a relaxed atmosphere, and will allow the brain extra focus for the complex thinking function.

Begin the exam with all of the questions with which the most confidence is felt. This will build the confidence level regarding the entire exam and will begin a quality momentum. This will also create encouragement for trying the problems where uncertainty resides.

Going with the "gut instinct" is always the way to go when solving a problem. Second guessing should be avoided at all costs. Have confidence in the ability to do well.

For essay questions, create an outline in advance that will keep the mind organized and make certain that all of the points are remembered. For multiple choice, read every answer, even if the correct one has been spotted - a better one may exist.

Continue at a pace that is reasonable and not rushed, in order to be able to work carefully. Provide enough time to go over the answers at the end, to check for small errors that can be corrected.

Should a feeling of panic begin, breathe deeply, and think of the feeling of the body releasing sand through its pores. Visualize a calm, peaceful place, and include all of the sights, sounds and sensations of this image. Continue the deep breathing, and take a few minutes to continue this with closed eyes. When all is well again, return to the test.

If a "blanking" occurs for a certain question, skip it and move on to the next question. There will be time to return to the other question later. Get everything done that can be done, first, to guarantee all the grades that can be compiled, and to build all of the confidence possible. Then return to the weaker questions to build the marks from there.

Remember, one's own reality can be created, so as long as the belief is there, success will follow. And remember: anxiety can happen later, right now, there's an exam to be written!

After the examination is complete, whether there is a feeling for a good grade or a bad grade, don't dwell on the exam, and be certain to follow through on the reward that was promised...and enjoy it! Don't dwell on any mistakes that have been made, as there is nothing that can be done at this point anyway.

Additionally, don't begin to study for the next test right away. Do something relaxing for a while, and let the mind relax and prepare itself to begin absorbing information again.

From the results of the exam - both the grade and the entire experience, be certain to learn from what has gone on. Perfect studying habits and work some more on confidence in order to make the next examination experience even better than the last one.

Learn to avoid places where openings occurred for laziness, procrastination and day dreaming.

Use the time between this exam and the next one to better learn to relax, even learning to relax on cue, so that any anxiety can be controlled during the next exam. Learn how to relax the body. Slouch in your chair if that helps. Tighten and then relax all of the different muscle groups, one group at a time, beginning with the feet and then working all the way up to the neck and face. This will ultimately relax the muscles more than they were to begin with. Learn how to breathe deeply and comfortably, and focus on this breathing going in and out as a relaxing thought. With every exhale, repeat the word "relax."

As common as test anxiety is, it is very possible to overcome it. Make yourself one of the test-takers who overcome this frustrating hindrance.

Additional Bonus Material

Due to our efforts to try to keep this book to a manageable length, we've created a link that will give you access to all of your additional bonus material.

Please visit http://www.mometrix.com/bonus948/series6 to access the information.